A Guide to Michigan's Endangered Wildlife

# A Guide to
# Michigan's Endangered Wildlife

David C. Evers

Ann Arbor
THE UNIVERSITY OF MICHIGAN PRESS

Copyright © by the University of Michigan 1992
All rights reserved
Published in the United States of America by
The University of Michigan Press
Manufactured in the United States of America

1995   1994   1993   1992      4   3   2   1


Library of Congress Cataloging-in-Publication Data

Evers, David C., 1962–
    A guide to Michigan's endangered wildlife / David C. Evers.
      p.      cm.
    Includes bibliographical references (p.   ).
    ISBN 0-472-08159-4 (paper: alk. paper)
    1. Endangered species—Michigan.   2. Wildlife conservation—
Michigan.   I. Title.
QL84.22.M5E94   1992
333.95′4137′09774—dc20                          91-36785
                                                    CIP

# Acknowledgments

THIS BOOK reflects the dedicated efforts of well over one hundred participants. Its beginnings were conceived in the offices of the Michigan Natural Features Inventory and arduously continued through five years of field research, extensive literature reviews, and numerous interviews with experts. The result is a book providing practical information that is easy to access. This is, however, just one contribution to a movement well underway to preserve endangered species and, eventually, ourselves.

The Michigan Department of Natural Resources Nongame Wildlife Fund (now part of the Natural Heritage Program), provided the baseline support for this project. The detailed maps are based on the extensive distributional work by researchers for the University of Michigan, Michigan Natural Features Inventory, and Michigan Breeding Bird Atlas. The Kalamazoo Nature Center also played a key role in this product, since it was a source of information and inspiration and furnished computer and office facilities, as well.

Wayne Miller, Bill Westrate, and Gerry Wykes deserve high recognition for their outstanding efforts in contributing, respectively, the butterfly, moth and miscellaneous insects, and mollusk (mussels and snails) accounts. Through a tedious and time-consuming process, Gail McPeek graciously reviewed and edited the book in its entirety, providing innumerable recommendations. John Eastman, Tom Weise, and Leni Wilsmann also contributed immeasurably with their reviews. The photographs featured here are the collected efforts of several professional photographers who have unselfishly provided their products for the "good of the cause." Carl Sams in particular deserves high recognition for his caring photographic support. Finally, I thank Mary Erwin, Christina Milton, and the rest of the University of Michigan Press staff for their dedication to this project.

We are grateful for the opportunity to include photographs from the following photographers:

Common loons, © Carl R. Sams II
Day-old eaglet, © Stephen Fettig
Cougar, © Carl R. Sams II
Lynx, © Larry Master
Marten, © Richard P. Smith
Gray wolf, © David Kenyon (MDNR)
Indiana bat, © Merlin D. Tuttle
Least shrew, © Fernando Cervantes-Reva
Prairie vole, © Lisa Davis and Lowell Getz
Common loon, © Carl R. Sams II
Least bittern, © Cortez Austin
Osprey, © Carl R. Sams II
Bald eagle, © Gijsbert van Frankenhuyzen (MDNR)
Red-shouldered hawk, © A. Morris (VIREO)
Merlin, © David P. Drummond
Merlin young, © Stephen Fettig
Peregrine falcon, © Richard P. Smith
Yellow rail, © Laura Lorenzetti Evers
King rail, © Robert H. Putnam
Piping plover, © Carl R. Sams II
Caspian tern, © Carl R. Sams II
Common tern, © M. P. Kahl (VIREO)
Barn owl, © Gijsbert van Frankenhuyzen (MDNR)
Long-eared owl, © Mike Dudash
Short-eared owl, © David Evers
Loggerhead shrike, © Steven Holt (VIREO)

Yellow-throated warbler, © Steven Holt (VIREO)
Kirtland's warbler, © D & M Zimmerman (VIREO)
Prairie warbler, © Steven Holt (VIREO)
Eastern fox snake, © Michigan Department of Natural Resources
Copperbelly water snake, © Alvin E. Staffan
Kirtland's snake, © Alvin E. Staffan
Marbled salamander, © Ohio Department of Natural Resources
Smallmouth salamander, © Ohio Department of Natural Resources
Lake sturgeon, © Bob Harrington
Pugnose minnow, © Alvin E. Staffan
Southern redbelly dace, © Alvin E. Staffan
Northern madtom, © Alvin E. Staffan
Duke's skipper, © Larry West
Northern blue, © Barbara Gerlach
Karner blue, © Morgens C. Nielsen
Leadplant moth, © Morgens C. Nielsen
American burying beetle line drawing, © Gerry Wykes
Bean villosa and northern rifleshell mussels, © Gerry Wykes
Cherrystone drop snail, © Gerry Wykes
Woodland caribou, © Carl R. Sams II
Lark sparrow, © Joe Kaplan
Wolverine, © Richard P. Smith

Cover illustration of trumpeter swans, © Carl R. Sams II.

# Contents

# Introduction

Michigan, a region endowed with an abundance of natural resources, is home to a wide variety of wildlife. This diversity reflects our surrounding natural wealth, the Great Lakes and their shorelines, the numerous inland lakes and streams, as well as extensive deciduous and coniferous forests. However, since the mid-1800s our assault on the environment has been far from respectful. Today, most of our natural resources, including wildlife, are treated callously, severely disrupting the delicate and interwoven nature of the ecosystems we all depend on. Former human-related problems associated with widespread logging and wetland destruction, the commercial harvest and persecution of wildlife, and unabated pollution of water, land, and air have been recognized. Nevertheless, various forms of these activities continue today, now accompanied by additional problems such as chemical contamination, intensive agriculture, and urban growth.

In response, Michigan passed the Endangered Species Act of 1974, finally recognizing the many wildlife species that were declining and in need of protection. When this law was enacted, a list of animals and plants was developed that identified species most gravely threatened with extinction in the state. By definition, endangered species are those designated as being in danger of extinction throughout all or a significant part of their range. Those species likely to become endangered in the foreseeable future are called threatened species.

Since 1974, the true status of selected species has been determined through studies and surveys. Therefore, the species included here are a realistic and relatively accurate picture of the endangered and threatened vertebrate wildlife in our state today (less is known about invertebrates). In 1991, 29 endangered and 49 threatened animals were protected under the Michigan Endangered Species Act.

Day-old Eaglet

This select group represents 7 mammals, 19 birds, 3 reptiles, 2 amphibians, and 19 fish. Invertebrates listed include 20 insects, 10 mussels, and 4 snails.

Since the Endangered Species Act's original enactment, a few species have disappeared from the state, such as the greater prairie chicken and lark sparrow. Other species have been removed from the list because their population and/or range has increased (such as the double-crested cormorant and Cooper's hawk), previously unknown populations have been discovered (such as the woodland vole), or their status was reassessed (such as the western lesser siren). Still others soon may be changed to extirpated status because populations have remained unknown for many years. Rediscovery of the following animals would be historic: least shrew, prairie vole, barn owl, bigeye chub, ironcolor shiner, pugnose minnow, weed shiner, river darter, regal fritillary, American burying beetle, lake floater, catspaw, and acorn rams-horn.

Although each species is profiled in the book, my presentation only begins to explain their complex life cycles and interrelationships with the environment. This book is not an identification guide or a comprehensive review of the species' biology and management. It will make you aware of wildlife needing immediate attention. It also describes what measures you can take to help ensure the survival of these species in Michigan. Distribution and population information is included to December, 1989. Population trends refer to changes in numbers and range during the 1980s. Estimated Michigan population numbers are for 1989.

Remember, endangered means there is still time. By working to solve environmental problems and supporting conservation, the long-term viability of species, their environments, and our own well-being as well, will be that much strengthened.

For questions, concerns, or reports regarding endangered and threatened animals, contact:

> Michigan Department of Natural Resources
> Natural Heritage Program
> Endangered Species Office
> P.O. Box 30028
> Lansing, MI 48909

# Mammals

MANY MAMMALS are common and are observed around our homes daily. Formerly, however, our mammalian diversity was greater and included species we would be hard-pressed to accept as Michigan residents. Wolverine and woodland caribou were scattered across the state, bison herds crossed over into our state's few prairie lands, and the eastern elk ranged throughout the Lower Peninsula. These species are now extirpated or extinct (in the case of the eastern elk subspecies). Other large mammals, such as the gray wolf, cougar, and lynx had widespread distributions but now are extremely rare and are precariously surviving in the northern regions of the state. Studies also show the loss of smaller species. Therefore, of the 68 known Michigan species, seven mammals are known to be currently threatened with extinction. The recovery of the once extirpated marten is a sign that we can reverse our past, short-sighted mistakes, however. Similar, intensive conservation efforts now need to be vigorously applied to our other missing mammalian fauna.

**Cougar** *(Felis concolor)*
Federal & State Endangered

Pop. Trend: Slightly increasing
Est. 1989 Michigan Pop.: 6–12

**Identification:** The cougar, also known as mountain lion or panther, is the only native Michigan cat with a long tail. Its large size (6 1/2–7 1/2 feet long), short tawny fur, lanky build, small head, and long curled tail are all characteristic of the cat. Adults weigh 80–200 pounds. Because of the cougar's very elusive nature, its presence is difficult to confirm. Signs, such as the 3–3 1/2 inch round tracks, large food caches, and scent posts are generally better methods for locating this cat.

**Range:** Once ranging from the Canadian Yukon south throughout the United States, this cat has experienced widespread declines in population and distribution. Two subspecies, the eastern cougar and Wisconsin puma are generally recognized as having occupied Michigan's Lower and Upper Peninsulas, respectively. Recently, this distinction has been challenged and the Upper Peninsula population is now considered to belong to the eastern cougar subspecies. This race is also believed to exist in scattered populations along the Appalachian Mountains north into Canada. Since the early 1900s, documentation of the Cougar's existence in Michigan has been inconclusive. However, annual sightings by experienced observers are frequently reported throughout the Upper Peninsula, and in 1985, a cougar was confirmed in Menominee County. Detailed sightings are most prevalent in the central Upper Peninsula, with recent indications of breeding in at least four counties; Delta, Marquette, Menominee, and Schoolcraft. An isolated and expanding cougar population has been recently discovered in southern Manitoba. Cougars are highly mobile creatures and individuals from this group have been dispersing into Minnesota and probably enter Michigan from Wisconsin.

**Habitat and Habits:** Being a large predator, the adaptive cougar is not dependent on specific habitats, but establishes its home range in extensive wooded areas with an abundant food supply. In the Great Lakes region, white-tailed deer are favored. It has been well documented that cougars kill proportionally more old and diseased deer in a regional population, resulting in a healthier and more stable deer herd. Adult cougars are solitary, except during the breeding season. The size of an established territory depends on season,

Map 1. Cougar. Distribution of observations of adults with young since 1985.

Cougar

prey availability, geographic location, and sex of the cougar. Den sites are typically located under fallen logs and brush. Following a three-month gestation period, an average litter of two to four kittens is born in the summer. The young are weaned two to three months after birth and remain with their mother for up to two years.

**Limiting Factors:** Human persecution led to the demise of the cougar in Michigan. In particular, predator control campaigns in the Great Lakes region led to the near extinction of this formerly widespread resident. Today and in the future, the cougar's reoccupation in Michigan hinges on public support.

**How to Help:** The cougar's existence in Michigan has been only recently confirmed. The small numbers of cougars in the state may be survivors from the past, transients from the western Great Lakes region, or privately released or escaped individuals. Whatever the case, the cougar does exist and it needs full protection. Report all sightings to the Michigan Department of Natural Resources (DNR) Endangered Species Office to allow investigation.

**Lynx** *(Felis lynx)*
State Endangered

Pop. Trend: Unknown
Est. 1989 Michigan Pop.: Unknown

**Identification:** This secretive cat, though quite similar to the more common bobcat, may be distinguished by its larger appearance; longer, black ear tufts; frosty gray fur; larger, furred feet; and stubbier tail. Its tail is completely black at the tip. Adult lynx are 30–42 inches long and weigh up to 40 pounds.

**Range:** The lynx occurs in northern forested regions worldwide. Its North American distribution once included much of the northern contiguous United States north to the Canadian-Alaskan treeline. In recent times, its distribution in both Michigan and the lower 48 states has severely declined. However, its wandering habits and periodic population upswings have provided a consistent flow of Canadian immigrant lynx into the Upper Peninsula. For instance, 12 lynx were taken in seven counties in 1962. This influx (part of an upper Great Lakes population irruption in 1961–63) has apparently allowed some recolonization of their northern Michigan range. This is encouraging since the lynx probably was extirpated in the early part of the century. Reminders of their secretive but definite presence are the occasional individuals caught by leghold traps. Rollin Baker, an authority on Michigan mammals, believes the lynx to be a "sustaining member of the outdoor community of the Upper Peninsula" in the early 1980s.

**Habitat and Habits:** This cat generally inhabits boreal evergreen forests. It adapts far less than the bobcat to forests disturbed by logging and clearing. The den site, chosen by the female, is a large hollow log or overturned stump; this shelters the litter of two to three kittens born in April or May. By July, the young are able to accompany their mother during hunting forays, and they remain with her through the winter. Lynx maintain large, distinct home ranges, with the males occupying 50–100 square miles. The lynx, with its proportionally long legs, snowshoelike foot pads, and great leaping ability, is well suited for capturing prey in snowbound regions. The cat's major prey is the snowshoe hare.

**Limiting Factors:** Past logging was extremely detrimental to the lynx. However, the human pressures that caused its original disappearance, hunting, trapping, and logging, are now less intense. The

Map 2. Lynx. Distribution of captured individuals since 1961.

Lynx

lynx is fully protected by law. Current timber practices of clear-cutting smaller areas may help the lynx, providing mature conifer stands remain intact. These cuts generally provide high densities of prey species. Threats that cast a shadow over the lynx's continued recovery include illegal poaching for furs, destruction of mature coniferous forests, and possible competition from the more adaptable bobcat. Periodic lynx population increases in Canada still contribute to Michigan's small and struggling population. However, this has not offset local mortality to make the lynx a prominent Michigan resident.

**How to Help:** Almost extinct by the middle of this century, the lynx has recently attempted to reclaim its Upper Peninsula range. To continue this upswing, individual animals must be rigorously protected and monitored. Lynx occasionally caught in leghold traps set for game species must be released, not destroyed. Landowners of mature forest tracts should try to preserve these areas and concentrate on developing second-growth stands for lumber or other needs. Stricter regulations are needed for Ontario's lynx harvest if the population in the northern Great Lakes region, including the Upper Peninsula, is to survive and expand. Report all observations of the lynx to the DNR Endangered Species Office.

**Marten** (*Martes americana*)
State Threatened

Pop. Trend: Increasing
Est. 1989 Michigan Pop.: Unknown

**Identification:** The marten resembles its relative, the smaller mink. It differs by its longer, yellowish brown fur, lighter head color, white-tipped ears, lack of a white chinstrap, and a distinct tannish chest patch. This member of the weasel family averages 14–17 inches long and weighs 1 1/2–2 3/4 pounds. Males are conspicuously larger than females.

**Range:** Before pioneer settlement, the marten inhabited boreal forests from the southern Rockies, upper Great Lakes region, and the Northeast north to the Arctic treeline. By the twentieth century, it had disappeared from much of its contiguous U.S. range, including the Upper and Lower Peninsulas of Michigan. Lingering individuals were occasionally seen, but an established population remained absent from Michigan until nearly 100 animals were released in the central Upper Peninsula in 1968–70. Since then, this population and other releases have recolonized much of the Upper Peninsula. A similar effort in the Pigeon River Country Forest Area and the Manistee National Forest in the northern Lower Peninsula also looks promising.

**Habitat and Habits:** Martens are generally associated with mature, upland coniferous forest throughout their range. In the eastern part, however, martens also use mixed conifer-hardwood stands, northern white cedar swamps, and sometimes open areas. The female marten establishes a den in a tree cavity or other protective hollow for the two to three young in March or April. Only the female cares for the young until they become relatively self-sufficient, approximately 11 weeks after birth. When the young are ready to leave the area, they may disperse 25 miles or more. These young, inexperienced martens are quite vulnerable to predators. The marten is generally active year-round, at twilight and night. They are adaptable hunters, feeding in trees for birds and on the ground for squirrels and for their primary prey, voles.

**Limiting Factors:** The marten's vulnerability to habitat destruction from logging and its susceptibility to trapping accounts for its demise in many parts of its range, including Michigan. Although heavily trapped in Michigan until the late 1800s, martens

Map 3. Marten. Distribution of individuals in 1989.

Marten

suffered their ultimate decline after the complete destruction of mature coniferous and mixed deciduous forest habitats. Recent efforts to reestablish the marten have met several difficulties, including their tendency to widely disperse. This thereby introduces greater mortality in unfamiliar places. However, protection of the animal and the gradual succession of pioneer plant communities to climax systems are helping the marten's recovery along.

**How to Help:** To improve marten habitat, forests must be managed to retain some old growth, particularly hemlock. The marten can coexist with small clear-cuts as long as heavily forested tracts are nearby. This furbearer is easily trapped, and until game seasons are established, the marten cannot be taken in Michigan. Always release trapped martens as soon as possible.

**Gray Wolf** (*Canis lupus*)
Federal & State Endangered

Pop. Trend: Slightly increasing
Est. 1989 Michigan Pop.: 20–25 individuals

**Identification:** The gray wolf, symbol of vast, untamed lands, is the largest member of the dog family. In the Great Lakes region it averages 5 feet in total length and weighs 60–80 pounds. Michigan wolves usually have a grizzled gray coat with a black shoulder mantle. Tracks, the most prominent indicators of wolf presence, vary greatly in size due to tracking conditions. Tracks measuring over 3 1/2 inches wide and 5 inches long that occur in relatively undisturbed areas may belong to a wolf. The long-drawn-out howls of a wolf differ from the short, "yip-yaps" of a coyote.

**Range:** While this canid may still be found throughout much of the northern hemisphere, North American wolves have been eliminated ever northward by human activity and unjustified, systematic slaughter. Today in the lower 48 states, wolves occur only in the northern Rockies, in northern Minnesota and Wisconsin, and in Michigan's Upper Peninsula and Isle Royale National Park. Isle Royale supports Michigan's only current viable population (12 in early 1989), since the Upper Peninsula wolf population remains widely scattered. Formation of a mainland pack occurred in early 1987 in Iron County for the first time since the late 1950s, but young were not produced. In 1989, several wolves were known along the Wisconsin-Michigan border and in or near Seney National Wildlife Refuge.

**Habitat and Habits:** The gray wolf has few specific habitat requirements other than its need for minimal human disturbance and extensive areas containing sufficient numbers of deer or moose. The wolf is a very social animal. It exhibits strong family ties such as the intricate pack hierarchy, where only the dominant male and female produce young. In early spring, four to ten pups are born. By October, the young of the year join the pack, fully maturing in two to three years. The pack structure is an important social unit, enabling the wolf to kill larger prey through cooperation. Weak, diseased, injured, and aged deer or moose, rather than healthy breeding individuals, are most likely to be taken by wolves. The gray wolf is an extremely shy animal, rarely seen even where it is present.

Map 4. Gray Wolf. Distribution of observations since 1977.

Gray Wolf

**Limiting Factors:** Until 1979, a major cause of wolf mortality was their accidental capture and destruction during the coyote bounty then in effect. This wasteful, ineffective predator control measure was repealed in that year. Today, the greatest threat to the struggling, small population of wolves in the Upper Peninsula is the antiwolf sentiments still held by a minority of the general public. These feelings are generally based upon myths and erroneous beliefs. Although the Isle Royale packs are protected, individual wolves that wander into the Upper Peninsula from Wisconsin and Ontario are deliberately killed before packs can form and produce young. A 1974 reintroduction project in the Upper Peninsula failed because of this type of antiwolf sentiment.

**How to Help:** Wolves are a crucially necessary component of a healthy ecosystem. Over the longterm, the populations of the species they prey upon are more balanced where a wolf pack is present. Michigan's Upper Peninsula contains several areas that could support wolf packs. Your active support of wolf restoration is needed. Immediately report any harassed wolves or their den sites to your local DNR field office or conservation officer. Except for Isle Royale observations, report all sightings to the DNR Endangered Species Office.

## Indiana Bat (*Myotis sodalis*)
Federal & State Endangered

Pop. Trend: Decreasing
Est. Michigan Pop.: Unknown

**Identification:** Identifying this bat species is very difficult. It requires an identification key and can be made only in-hand. In general, this relatively small bat has dark, brownish fur and wing membranes and short, rounded ears. Its average total body length is 3 1/2 inches.

**Range:** Indiana bats summer throughout much of the eastern United States as individuals in maternity colonies, as transients, or as wanderers. In winter, however, the majority of the population (85 percent) congregates in only seven known caves, located in Missouri, Kentucky, and Indiana. Hibernation lasts six months. Surveys in these caves show a 50 percent decline since 1960. In Michigan, before intensive surveys in 1978 and 1979, there were only nine known records, each in the southern three tiers of counties in the Lower Peninsula. By 1980, nearly twice this number had been caught by mist nets in four southern Michigan counties. Several were lactating females, the first solid evidence that Indiana bats reproduce in the state. The Thornapple River in Eaton County supported the highest concentration of captures. Since those surveys, no further observations of this little-studied species have been recorded.

**Habitat and Habits:** During winter, Indiana bats hibernate exclusively in caves and mines south of the Michigan border. In May, the Indiana bat migrates to Michigan and forms colonies near stream and river floodplains. The bats usually locate the nursery roost sites beneath loose bark or in tree hollows adjacent to these waterways. The Indiana bat does not use buildings or other structures for any part of its life cycle. After the female gives birth to a single offspring in June or July, females and young join to form nursery colonies, which may be repeatedly used in successive years. Warm temperatures in early summer are crucial to the growth and success of each year's progeny. Normally, the young are able to fly one month after birth. Like most bats, the Indiana bat is most active during twilight and nighttime hours, using echolocation to avoid obstacles and find prey. Indiana bats typically feed on flying insects, preferably moths, over waterways.

Map 5. Indiana Bat. Distribution of captured individuals since 1978.

Indiana bat

**Limiting Factors:** Although the 1987 total population was estimated at 260,000, the Indiana bat's habit of gathering in only a few caves makes the entire species vulnerable to a catastrophy. The winter hibernating quarters are subject to floods, ceiling collapses, vandals, and other disturbances. In Michigan, the Indiana bat is affected by deforestation of streamside habitats, including cutting large dead trees for firewood. Pesticide contamination of insect prey have caused substantial mortality in some U.S. bat colonies and also may affect the Indiana bat.

**How to Help:** In Michigan, this bat can be helped by protecting wooded river and stream areas and retaining large, dead trees. Further research is needed on the specific summer habitat requirements of this species, the effects of floodplain habitat destruction, the effects of water pollution and siltation, and the influence of pesticides.

**Least Shrew** (*Cryptotis parva*)  Pop. Trend: Unknown
**Prairie Vole** (*Microtus ochrogaster*)  Est. Michigan Pop.: Unknown
State Threatened (both)

**Identification:** In general, shrews are identified by their pointed nose, elongated head, and small eyes. The least shrew, one of Michigan's smallest mammals (2–2 1/2 inches long), has a brownish back and short tail (1/2–3/4 inches). Voles have small ears, a short tail, brown to gray fur, and rodentlike incisors. The presence of voles can be detected by runways formed in grassy areas. The prairie vole has few visual features to distinguish it from other voles. Adults average 4 1/2 inches in body length with a tail about one-third of this length (less than 1 1/2 inches). The commonly associated meadow vole typically has a tail length greater than 1 1/2 inches.

**Range:** The least shrew is most common in the southeastern United States, with Michigan serving as its northern range boundary. This species probably occurred throughout much of the southern Lower Peninsula, but there are only 12 counties with confirmed records. Most were collected between the early and mid-1900s, with the last Michigan record in 1960. However, this diminutive mammal could be rediscovered in southern locales through small mammal sampling surveys. Primarily a rodent of the Great Plains, the prairie vole has an even more restricted Michigan range. This species was first recorded in Michigan in 1918. While it may have been a recent invader, the oak savannas and scattered prairies present before European settlement would have provided suitable habitat. The prairie vole has been documented in 4 counties in extreme southwestern Michigan and was last confirmed in 1961 in Kalamazoo County.

**Habitat and Habits:** Seeming to adapt to a variety of open habitats, including wet meadows, fallow fields, and forest edges, the least shrew has, nevertheless, disappeared from many areas. Minimally disturbed grasslands may be the most preferred habitat. The least shrew is social and may gather in communal nests during winter months. Its breeding period extends from early spring to late autumn, producing up to three litters of three to six young yearly. Insects are the main items in its diet. Prairie voles also inhabit open areas, sometimes hay fields. It is commonly found with the meadow vole, a closely related species with similar behavioral characteristics. This vole is primarily a grazer, eating any plant material, in-

Least Shrew

Map 6. Least Shrew and Prairie Vole. Historical distribution of captured individuals.

Prairie Vole

cluding seeds and roots. A female can annually produce five litters, each containing two to six young. This high reproductive potential results in periodic population fluctuations.

**Limiting Factors:** Very few Michigan studies of these small mammals have been done. Both are at the periphery of their range and generally depend on minimally disturbed grasslands for self-sustaining populations. Direct mortality and contamination of their food supply caused by pesticides may be related to their decline.

**How to Help:** Studies or surveys to locate and document these species are desperately needed. One fairly simple method is to dissect owl and hawk pellets, searching for skulls or jaw bones. Report any information to the DNR Endangered Species Office.

# Birds

APPROXIMATELY four hundred species of birds are confirmed in Michigan (235 nesting species). This ever-increasing number is not the result of an improving environment; rather, it is due to the swelling ranks of birders and other observers depending on the wandering mobility of birds. For example, only 309 birds were listed in Michigan by 1943. Paralleling this increase in sightings is the number of endangered and threatened birds, now totaling 19 species (plus 3 that are extirpated and 1 that is extinct). Popularity and intense conservation efforts have helped some species, such as the bald eagle and peregrine falcon, to recover. However, the continued loss of wetland and grassland habitats, increasing recreational activity on beaches and lakes, and various chemical contaminants severely impact these rare species and are causing population declines in others.

**Common Loon** (*Gavia immer*)
State Threatened

Pop. Trend: Slightly decreasing
Est. 1989 Michigan Pop.: 270–300
breeding pairs

**Identification:** The common loon, known for its wilderness mystique and familiar laughing, tremolo call, also has a distinct appearance. It has a long body, black-and-white checkered back, dark head, a daggerlike, black bill, and sloping forehead. Adults have a wingspan of 5 feet and average 32 inches long. Although there is no plumage difference between sexes, only the male makes the territorial yodel call. In winter, adults and young wear similar plumage of drab gray and white.

**Range:** Unlike the world's other four loon species, the common loon is restricted to North America and Iceland. It breeds from the northernmost reaches of the continent south to the northern Rocky Mountains in the west, and east through the northern Great Lakes region and New England. While the northern Great Lakes continues to support sizable populations, breeding loons in Michigan have largely disappeared from the southern Lower Peninsula and have experienced over a 50 percent decline in the eastern Upper Peninsula. Northern Michigan population densities are in Isle Royale, the western Upper Peninsula, and Seney National Wildlife Refuge. Remnant pairs tenuously survive in the southern Lower Peninsula in Barry, Montcalm, and southern Newaygo counties. Thousands of northbound loons migrate through Michigan, where peninsulas such as Whitefish Point provide optimal opportunities to see large concentrations. This waterbird winters along the Gulf and Atlantic coasts.

**Habitat and Habits:** In April, loons begin to move north into Michigan's forested lakes. Nesting pairs are selective, typically preferring lakes larger than 40 acres that contain small islands. Males typically arrive before the females. Loons construct their nests within a few feet of the water's edge to allow for a quick underwater exit. A pair usually produces two black, down-covered chicks that are led to a shallow cove for 8 to 12 weeks. Before their southward migration, loons congregate on the Great Lakes until November. Loons are opportunistic feeders, but depend primarily upon a variety of fish up to 8 inches long. Prey, including crayfish, are caught during 30- to-60-second dives.

Map 7. Common Loon. Distribution of breeding pairs in 1989.

Common Loon

**Limiting Factors:** Several human-related pressures are affecting our Michigan common loon populations. These include direct mortality by commercial fishing nets and the less apparent effects of chemical contamination. Acid rain, organochlorines, dieldrin, dioxins, and heavy metals such as mercury all contribute to increasing pressures on the loon's survival. The loon's vulnerability to disturbance of its nesting territory makes shoreline development and recreational use of lakes a severe problem. During migration, loons are weakened by the accumulation of mercury in their bodies, thus becoming more susceptible to such diseases as avian botulism.

**How to Help:** Common loon pairs are very sensitive to human disturbance of their nesting and nursery areas. Activities should be kept at least 500 feet from a nest. Harassment or unintentional disturbance can usually be avoided by forming community watches. On lakes with fluctuating water levels or those lacking suitable island or shoreline nesting habitat, 16-square-foot artificial floating platforms can be anchored in sheltered areas of the lake. Consult knowledgeable groups before platform placement to avoid attracting loons to marginal areas.

**Least Bittern** (*Ixobrychus exilis*)  Pop. Trend: Stable
State Threatened                      Est. 1989 Michigan Pop.: Unknown

**Identification:** Inconspicuous and secretive, the least bittern is difficult to observe unless flushed into flight. Look for its dangling legs, quick wing beats, outstretched neck, and chestnut-colored wing patches. The overall rufous coloring, black head and back, and small size (11–14 inches long) further identify it. During the breeding season, three to five "coos" are repeated at frequent intervals.

**Range:** The least bittern's extensive range includes parts of North, Central, and South America. In North America, it is mostly restricted to the eastern United States, although isolated nesting populations do occur in California, Arizona, and New Mexico. Its northern range periphery includes parts of southern Canada. In Michigan, this is generally a heron of the Lower Peninsula, although disjunct colonies are known in the Upper Peninsula. Nest records are known for about one-third of Michigan's counties. Intensive and widespread surveys since the early 1980s indicate a decline in distribution and abundance. However, the least bittern remains a viable component in many wetland ecosystems in the southern Lower Peninsula and in wetlands associated with the Lake Michigan shoreline. This heron migrates south of the Michigan border, wintering along the Atlantic and Gulf coasts from Florida and Texas south into Mexico.

**Habitat and Habits:** This marsh dweller inhabits dense cattail and bulrush wetlands interspersed with patches of open water. Nesting areas are invariably over water, usually no deeper than 3 feet. Spring and autumn foraging sites are characterized by shallower water, and vegetation typically ranges from 2 to 4 feet high. Least bitterns arrive in the southern Lower Peninsula in mid-May. Nest platforms are built with an overhanging canopy of vegetation, usually 1/2 to 2 1/2 feet above water. Egg laying extends from May through July. An average of four to five eggs are incubated 17–20 days. Young wander from the nest at 5–9 days, frequently returning for several weeks. Most individuals have left Michigan by early September. As expected, aquatic organisms are a prominent part of its diet, including small fish, tadpoles, crayfish, dragonflies, and other insects.

Map 8. Least Bittern. Distribution of breeding pairs in 1989.

Least Bittern

**Limiting Factors:** Habitat loss is the overriding factor in the least bittern's decline, not surprising since over 70 percent of Michigan's wetlands have been destroyed or altered. This loss does not fully explain the decline, however. Known colonies have disappeared, despite extensive areas of apparently suitable habitat. Suspected contributors to its decline are environmental contaminants, unnaturally high densities of predators (such as raccoons) and general wetland quality degradation, frequently related to changes in water flows.

**How to Help:** Protection and management of occupied wetlands is required for self-sustaining populations. Relatively large cattail stands of at least 15 acres interspersed with open water are suitable sites for nesting pairs. Quality control of wetlands is also crucial. Avoid disturbing buffering shoreline vegetation, disrupting water levels, and dumping chemicals nearby. All wetlands larger than 5 contiguous acres are vigorously protected by the Michigan Wetland Protection Act of 1979.

**Osprey** (*Pandion haliaetus*)
State Threatened

Pop. Trend: Increasing
Est. 1989 Michigan Pop.: 169 breeding pairs

**Identification:** Known to many lakeshore residents as the "fish hawk," the osprey is easily identified with dark brown above, white below, and a mostly white head with a broad, black cheek-band. These birds, with their 6-foot wingspan, often fly with an angle in the elbow of the long, narrow wings, showing the telltale black wrist patches on the underwing.

**Range:** Like the peregrine falcon and barn owl, the osprey has a cosmopolitan range. In North America, it occurs from Canada south to the northern United States and along both coasts. Rebounding from a record low of 51 known occupied nests in 1965, the osprey is now approaching former numbers and distribution in the state. Michigan's osprey population is most concentrated in the eastern Upper Peninsula and on selected floodings, such as Fletcher's Pond in Alpena and Montmorency counties of the northern Lower Peninsula. This raptor winters south of Michigan into Central and South America.

**Habitat and Habits:** This bird of prey occurs in forested regions in the vicinity of lakes, large rivers, and floodings. Ospreys build an extremely large nest in a prominent tree, and frequently return to the same site year after year. Artificial structures, such as utility poles, also are used. An average of three eggs are laid from late April to early June. The female is primarily responsible for incubation, while the male fishes for both. Eggs hatch in about five weeks and the young can fly after seven weeks of age. Immature osprey remain on the wintering grounds during their first full summer. By the third year, individuals generally return north to search for a nesting site. Optimal feeding areas for this strict fish-eater are clear, shallow waters free from floating and submerged vegetation. Favored prey, such as bullhead, yellow perch, crappie, and sunfish, are easier to locate in these conditions.

**Limiting Factors:** Since the 1950s, persistent pollutants such as DDT are documented as being the leading factor for major osprey population declines. These chemicals were proven to cause reproductive failure due to thin eggshells that break during incubation.

Map 9. Osprey. Distribution of breeding pairs in 1989.

Osprey

Since the ban of DDT and other organic pesticides, osprey populations have rebounded. Seclusion during the nesting period is critical, and the adults will desert an overexposed or disturbed nest. There is some concern that acid rain may become a problem due to its severe effect on fish populations.

**How to Help:** As with bald eagle populations, the DNR annually conducts intensive surveys of the osprey to monitor its status, nesting success, and population trends. At existent osprey nest sites, a minimally disturbed safety zone of 300 feet is generally necessary. However, the amount of isolation depends on the resident pair's tolerance level. In areas with suitable foraging habitat, tripod-type nesting platforms can be erected to attract osprey pairs. Consult a natural resources organization before placement.

**Bald Eagle** (*Haliaeetus leucocephalus*)
Federal & State Threatened

Pop. Trend: Increasing
Est. 1989 Michigan Pop.: 165
breeding pairs

**Identification:** The conspicuous white head and tail of the adult, contrasting with its dark brown body, and its 6–7 foot wingspan sets the bald eagle apart from all other Michigan birds. Immature bald eagles, although easy to confuse with the migratory, golden eagle, may be most reliably identified by their white, upper-wing linings. In flight, the bald eagle soars with a flat, horizontal wing profile.

**Range:** The bald eagle's breeding range formerly extended from Alaska and central Canada south into the southern United States. Major breeding concentrations in the contiguous United States are centered in the western Great Lakes basin, Maine, Chesapeake Bay, Florida, and the Pacific Northwest. Small, scattered populations and several on-going release programs continue to expand North America's increasing population. In Michigan, the bald eagle population is beginning to recover from its decline throughout the state. Since 1987, two pairs have resided in the Saginaw Bay region and pairs have attempted to nest in Allegan and Monroe counties. Although chemical pollution remains at high levels in Great Lakes shoreline habitats, nesting pairs have reestablished along these areas. The western Upper Peninsula contains the densest breeding population. Many of Michigan's nesting bald eagles remain in the state during winter.

**Habitat and Habits:** Michigan's bald eagles arrive on their nesting territories from mid-February to mid-March. Pairs proceed to re-build the massive stick nests commonly used year after year. Preferred nest sites are near the top of large, living trees, often on prominent points near lakes, rivers, or floodings that have an adequate supply of fish. Elaborate "cartwheel" courtship displays occur before the laying of two, pure white eggs. Incubation lasts about 35 days. Paired adults, which mate for life, attend the dependent young for three to four months. Bald Eagles reach maturity and acquire their diagnostic white head and tail plumage in about four years.

**Limiting Factors:** Several conditions have contributed to the bald eagle's threatened status. Foremost was the widespread use of

Map 10. Bald Eagle. Distribution of breeding pairs in 1989.

Bald Eagle

organochlorine pesticides, especially DDT. This chemical severely affected eagle production by reducing the shell thickness of eggs, resulting in breaking. These pesticides are now banned or their use is significantly reduced, and eagle populations are responding with increases in numbers and range. Threats that affect nesting success include human disturbance during the first 12 weeks of the nesting cycle; continued chemical contamination; lead poisoning; general habitat destruction, such as shoreline development; and, to a lesser extent, shooting, incidental trapping, and the indirect effects of acid rain.

**How to Help:** Locations of Michigan bald eagle nest sites are recorded and monitored each year by the DNR, thereby reducing accidental disturbance of nests and their associated territories. Human activity during the breeding season should be kept at a minimum of 300 feet from the nest tree. Although protecting bald eagles and their habitat is critically important, nesting populations can be restored with young eagles using various release techniques. Support from local groups can initiate such projects.

# Red-Shouldered Hawk

*(Buteo lineatus)*

State Threatened

Pop. Trend: Slightly decreasing

Est. 1989 Michigan Pop.: 100–150 breeding pairs

**Identification:** As an adult, this colorful raptor's reddish shoulder, checkered back pattern, and rufous barred underparts make it easy to identify. Like all hawks in the *Buteo* family, the red-shouldered has a wide, rounded tail and broad wings. You can quickly distinguish the red-shouldered in flight by the crescent-shaped "windows" near the wing tips. Immature birds are heavily streaked with brown teardrop markings on their underparts. Red-shouldereds have a variable wingspan of 3–4 feet and may measure 17–24 inches long.

**Range:** Two separate geographic populations of red-shouldered hawks occur in North America: a western population restricted to California, and a widely distributed eastern one. Our eastern population is exhibiting a long-term decline. Widespread and abundant in southern Michigan until the 1940s, this hawk has now been pushed to marginal habitats in the northern Lower Peninsula. Concentrations are known in the Manistee River Valley and Cheboygan and Alpena counties. In addition, pairs are increasingly moving north into the Upper Peninsula, where the first confirmed nesting was in 1978. Since 1983, 14 southern Michigan counties have recorded its presence during the breeding season. However only 5 of those counties have confirmed its nesting in a region where it was once the most common *Buteo*. Some individual birds winter in the southern counties, but most move south of the state.

**Habitat and Habits:** Late February and early March brings the first red-shouldered pairs to southern Michigan. While their traditionally preferred habitat is mature floodplain forest, this hawk has adapted to northern Michigan's upland mixed forests, especially those adjacent to water. In their stick nest, typically placed in a large tree in or below the leaf canopy, both parents incubate three to four eggs for almost a month, beginning in early to mid-April. The young fledge at about six weeks but remain dependent on their parents for several more weeks. Red-shouldered hawks usually obtain most of their prey, reptiles, amphibians, and small rodents, from wetland areas interspersed within mature forests.

Map 11. Red-shouldered Hawk. Distribution of breeding pairs since 1983.

Red-shouldered Hawk

**Limiting Factors:** The red-shouldered hawk is extremely susceptible to disturbances of its floodplain forest habitat. Although clear-cut logging has the obvious effect of reducing suitable areas of habitat, selective cutting can also restrict breeding pairs from developing territories in more subtle ways. Such changes stimulate new understory growth and deteriorate otherwise suitable red-shouldered habitat by making it less attractive to them, though more appealing to the highly adaptable red-tailed hawk, an aggressive competitor. Low nest-production rates in the northern Lower Peninsula may result from marginal breeding habitat, greater climate extremes, and low prey availability.

**How to Help:** Moderating the decline of red-shouldered hawks, especially in the southern Lower Peninsula, requires preserving existing floodplain forests and wet, mature, wooded areas. The extent of mature forest required for a successful pair is 250–600 acres. Interspersed openings, preferably wet meadows, should comprise about 20 percent of the suitable habitat. A distance of at least 300 feet from the nest should be kept free of human disturbance. Report all southern Lower Peninsula nest sites to the DNR Endangered Species Office.

**Merlin** (*Falco columbarius*)
State Threatened

Pop. Trend: Increasing
Est. 1989 Michigan Pop.: 35–60
breeding pairs

**Identification:** Identify the merlin, a medium-sized falcon (11 inches long, 24-inch wingspan), by its long, pointed wings, its long, barred tail, and its vertically streaked underparts. The bird's faint "sideburns" are much lighter than those of the similar, but much larger, peregrine falcon. Adult males, with their blue-gray backs differ markedly from the brown adult females and immatures.

**Range:** This quick-flying falcon resides throughout the Northern Hemisphere, including the boreal forest of Alaska and Canada south to the northern contiguous United States. In Michigan, however, the merlin has always been a rare breeding bird restricted to the Upper Peninsula. Its local and elusive summer occurrence hampers accurate assessment of its population status, indicated by its first confirmed nesting in 1955. However, recent migration and summer field observations show a significant upward trend. At least eight Upper Peninsula counties have confirmed nesting, with high nesting densities in Isle Royale National Park and the Keweenaw Peninsula. Summer sightings of territorial pairs are rare but increasing in the northern Lower Peninsula. Merlins migrate throughout the state and may be best observed in the spring at Whitefish Point. Most merlins winter south of Michigan into Central and South America.

**Habitat and Habits:** For nesting sites, Michigan merlins typically favor spruce or other conifers near bogs or open water. Large pines adjacent to the Lake Superior shoreline are excellent nesting areas for this falcon. The four to five eggs are laid by early June in an old raven, crow, or hawk nest (falcons do not build their own nests). Both parents aggressively defend the young, and the immature birds are independent nine weeks after hatching. By November, most merlins have migrated south of the state. Major movements of this predatory bird usually correlate with the migration of small birds. In summer, birds as well as large insects such as dragonflies are taken. The merlin ambushes its prey either from a perch or in flight.

**Limiting Factors:** Like other birds of prey, the merlin occupies the top of the food chain. Therefore, it is susceptible to contamination

Map 12. Merlin. Distribution of breeding pairs in 1989.

Merlins

by accumulated chemicals such as DDT and other organochlorines. Currently, destructive chemicals are not known to seriously threaten the merlin's breeding success in the Great Lakes region. The merlin may, however, be exposed to high levels of pesticides in its South American wintering grounds. Illegal shooting and other direct mortality from humans has been minimized (as it has for most other raptors in Michigan).

**How to Help:** Recently, the population increases of crows and ravens in northern Michigan have provided a greater number of available nesting sites for this falcon. This may be partially responsible for the merlin's recent population increase in the upper Great Lakes region. Therefore, a possible technique to further help the merlin is to provide platforms in tall conifers adjacent to large bodies of water.

## Peregrine Falcon
*(Falco peregrinus)*
Federal & State Endangered

Pop. Trend: Increasing
Est. 1989 Michigan Pop.: 1 breeding
pair

**Identification:** Known and admired for its swift flight, the peregrine falcon is a crow-sized bird of prey with long, pointed wings (15–20 inch wingspan). Adults are slate-gray backed with light, streaked underparts and a black head. A distinct feature of the peregrine is its dark sideburns. Immatures are brown with prominent streaking on the breast. The flight is quick with rapid wingbeats, although migrating peregrines soar for extended periods.

**Range:** Nearly worldwide in distribution, the peregrine falcon originally nested throughout much of North America. In the 1940s, an estimated 350 pairs were present in the eastern United States. But by the mid-1960s, the peregrine was declining throughout the country and had completely disappeared east of the Mississippi. This abrupt and alarming change in its status spearheaded captive breeding projects and releases. Today, nesting peregrines have returned to many eastern states. Historically, Michigan's population was confined to northern Michigan with only ten nest sites known. The last confirmed Michigan nesting pair was in 1957 along the Garden Peninsula shoreline in Delta County. Beginning in 1986, peregrines have been released in two urban environs, Grand Rapids and Detroit. Releases at natural sites began in 1988 on Isle Royale and in the Ottawa National Forest. In the following year, Pictured Rocks National Lakeshore joined these two sites and also "hacked out" birds. In 1989, for the first time in over three decades, a Michigan nesting pair of peregrine falcons established a territory and laid eggs. The pair used a downtown building in Detroit. A total of 96 peregrines were released in the Upper Midwest in 1989, promising further improvements in Michigan's nesting population. The peregrine winters along the Atlantic Coast into South America.

**Habitat and Habits:** Peregrines prefer nesting sites on high cliffs or artificial structures overlooking water and other open areas. Available prey is crucial to nesting success. This raptor requires large concentrations of waterfowl or colonies of gulls and other birds such as pigeons during the production of young. Urban areas with high-rise buildings and bridges and an abundant food supply attract peregrine pairs. In spring, a pair chooses a nest site (eyrie) and incubates

Map 13. Peregrine Falcon. Historic distribution of breeding pairs.

Peregrine Falcon

three to four eggs for around one month. Young falcons can fly five to six weeks after hatching. Adults and their young return annually to the same nest site if nesting conditions are favorable. Young peregrines begin to breed at two to three years of age.

**Limiting Factors:** The overwhelming cause for this falcon's catastrophic decline was the high use of organochlorine pesticides (such as DDT). The peregrine falcon retains one of the highest levels of DDT residues of all vertebrates, which led to reproductive failures due to eggshell thinning. Since the U.S. ban of DDT in 1972, peregrines have slowly recovered to former population levels. Restoration efforts in the wild, just underway, have to take into account prey density and predation of peregrine falcon young by the great horned owl. But, hopes are high for an established nesting population in the Upper Peninsula in the next few years.

**How to Help:** Public support for reestablishing this species is high and is a major reason for project funding. Awareness of the effects of organic pesticides has improved, although many chemical contaminants are still liberally applied. Report sightings of peregrine falcons during the summer to the DNR Endangered Species Office.

# Yellow Rail

(*Coturnicops noveboracensis*)
State Threatened

Pop. Trend: Stable
Est. 1989 Michigan Pop.: 60–80
breeding pairs

**Identification:** Highly sought by birders, the secretive yellow rail is indeed a unique discovery in Michigan. Rarely observed, it generally is found by its rhythmic and continuous ticking calls. Peak calling bouts are restricted to nighttime hours between early May and late June. Calls can be easily imitated by the hitting of two stones together in an alternating series of "tic-tic, tic-tic-tic." When viewed, notice its small size (6–7 1/2 inches in length), overall buff-yellow coloration with frost-edged back feathers. When flushed, its flight pattern appears weak; in daylight a pronounced wing patch is apparent.

**Range:** Locally distributed across interior Canada, the breeding range of the yellow rail barely crosses the U.S. border. Its U.S. populations are most regular and contiguous in the northern Great Lakes Region, particularly Minnesota. Although there are historical breeding records in southern Michigan, the yellow rail's few strongholds currently exist in the Upper Peninsula. Known sites include Munuscong Bay in Chippewa County, Sleeper Lake in Luce County, and the Seney National Wildlife Refuge (NWR) in Schoolcraft County. This latter site contains the largest population in Michigan; 52 calling males were found in 1982. Since the mid- to late 1980s, rails also have been found in other Luce and Schoolcraft County locales, in Alger County, and near Houghton Lake, Roscommon County. Spring and autumn migrants occasionally occur throughout the state. It winters along the ocean coast from North Carolina to Texas.

**Habitat and Habits:** In Michigan, the yellow rail is nearly exclusively restricted to extensive wet openings dominated by stands of sedge (particularly *Carex lasiocarpa*). In these wetlands, standing water of several inches, matlike dead vegetation (not sphagnum moss), and minimal woody vegetation are crucial. Males return to the breeding grounds in early to mid-May. Egg laying begins in late May and may continue through the end of June (including re-nesting). Only the female incubates the six to ten eggs, evidently for 17–18 days, within a sedge-canopy nest. The black, downy feathered young leave the nest within 1 day. This rail feeds on available invertebrates and vegetation.

Map 14. Yellow Rail. Distribution of breeding pairs in 1989.

Yellow Rail

**Limiting Factors:** The yellow rail's stringent habitat requirements limit its distribution in Michigan. This, coupled with natural succession and widespread wetland destruction, necessitates current occupied sites to be monitored and long-term management plans developed. The Munuscong Bay population may be gone due to severe habitat alteration. Other sites, however, are nestled in wilderness conditions and currently are little threatened by human disturbance. Natural water level fluctuation and fires are crucial for maintaining sedge meadow habitat.

**How to Help:** Two occupied sites, Sleeper Lake and Seney National Wildlife Refuge are protected. Surveys are needed to document additional sites; search sedge meadows after sunset between mid-May and June. Listen for rhythmic ticking calls; the sound of several males at a distance closely resembles a typewriter. Imitated ticking calls elicit aggressive responses by males.

**King Rail** (*Rallus elegans*)
State Endangered

Pop. Trend: Stable
Est. 1989 Michigan Pop.: 20–35
breeding pairs

**Identification:** This large, rust-colored, slender marsh bird, twice the size of the more common and familiar Virginia rail, has a laterally compressed body that is well suited for escaping danger through thick marsh vegetation. When flushed, its short, seemingly weak flight seldom carries it far. The average length of adults is 15–19 inches and the wingspan is 21–25 inches. The king rail is often detected by its grunting or staccato calls.

**Range:** Although the king rail breeds from the Great Lakes region to the Atlantic Coast and south to the Gulf Coast and Cuba, it is most prevalent in marsh-rice belts of the southern states and freshwater marshes associated with the Atlantic Coast. The Michigan breeding range of this elusive rail was once widespread from Saginaw Bay and Muskegon, south. Wanderers have been reported as far north as the Upper Peninsula. Today, viable populations are generally restricted to Lake Erie marshes and the St. Clair Flats—areas that historically contained the greatest densities. Saginaw Bay and River wetlands, Nayanquing Point, and southern Michigan inland marshes harbor pairs or small populations. Great Lakes' populations may be found wintering along the Atlantic Coast in the southern United States.

**Habitat and Habits:** In Michigan, this rail prefers large, permanent marsh systems with cattail stands, sedge-grass tussocks, or herbaceous marsh vegetation interspersed with willows and dogwoods. Arriving Michigan king rails establish territories in late April. Following a courtship strutting display, the birds choose a nest site in a clump of vegetation, incubating the 10 to 11 eggs for around three weeks. After hatching, the black young quickly vacate the nest. Survival rate of the young is about 50 percent for the first two weeks. After that it increases with age. The king rail sometimes feeds on insects in upland areas adjacent to marshes, but it typically prefers small crustaceans, fish, frogs, and aquatic insects found in 2–3 inches of water.

**Limiting Factors:** The king rail's Midwest breeding population is declining, probably because of severe wetland loss, lead poisoning,

Map 15. King Rail. Distribution of breeding pairs since 1986.

King Rail

and high pesticide residue levels in their habitat. Though specific reasons for their decline are not fully understood, these factors further stress a population already constrained by its marginal range. Michigan's migratory king rail population also may be geographically isolated from the more abundant, stationary southern populations. If so, any future increase of this species in the Midwest depends on the productivity within its own population. Natural predators include the raccoon, which exists in abnormally high densities throughout the southern Lower Peninsula.

**How to Help:** The large, marshy expanses required by king rails continue to decline throughout the state. Conservation of this decimated habitat and support for Michigan's Wetland Protection Act are ways to help. For landowners, quality habitat management includes enhancing marshes by manipulating water levels and vegetation density. Artificial nesting platforms may help this rail. These structures are successfully used by a close relative, the clapper rail. Report all observations of king rails to the DNR Endangered Species Office.

## Piping Plover

*(Charadrius melodus)*
Federal & State Endangered

Pop. Trend: Slightly decreasing
Est. 1989 Michigan Pop.: 17–19
breeding pairs

**Identification:** Recognize this diminutive plover by its pale, sand-colored back and head, white rump, orange legs, and single, black breast band. Adults measure about 7 inches long, with a 15-inch wingspan. Cryptic coloration makes piping plovers difficult to see. But, as its name implies, it often gives away its location by its insistent piping call, a sound similar to "peep" or "peep-lo."

**Range:** The piping plover occupies three main breeding regions: the north and middle Atlantic coast, the Great Lakes basin, and the Great Plains region. The latter holds the largest remaining populations. In Michigan, this plover was once common along the Lake Michigan and Lake Huron shorelines, with estimates ranging as high as 150–200 pairs in 18 counties. In 1979, only 33 nesting pairs were found, followed by a 50 percent decrease to 17 pairs in 1981. Since then, the population has fluctuated between 14 and 20 pairs. Some of the breeding population has now shifted to marginal habitat on Lake Superior beaches, although a few pairs continue to survive along historical nesting beaches on northern Lake Michigan shorelines and islands. The Michigan pairs represent the entire Great Lakes population. Piping plovers winter on the Gulf and Atlantic coasts. Recent band recoveries indicate Michigan's population winters along the Florida Coast.

**Habitat and Habits:** In the Great Lakes region, the piping plover prefers to nest and forage on sandy beaches sprinkled with pebbles, containing sparse or no vegetation. The average preferred beach width is 100 feet. For its nest, the bird scrapes a shallow depression in the sand and pebbles between the water's edge and the foredune. By mid- to late May it lays a clutch of four eggs. The young birds leave the nest only hours after hatching, but they remain under their parents' protection and fully fledge after three to four weeks. Insects and other invertebrates are staples of the plover's diet. Favored foraging areas are lakeshore margins, shallow dune pools, and streams flowing into the Great Lakes.

**Limiting Factors:** The piping plover is extremely sensitive to the type and degree of disturbance on its sandy nesting beaches, areas

Map 16. Piping Plover. Distribution of breeding pairs in 1989.

Piping Plover

in which human recreational use has grown tremendously in the past several decades. Activities and other factors that disturb nesting plovers include (1) people in the breeding territory, (2) free-roaming dogs, (3) off road vehicles (ORVs), (4) loss of nesting habitat through beach erosion, rising lake levels, inclement weather, and plant succession, and (5) predation by increasing numbers of gulls, crows, and raccoons. In addition, hazards during migration and on its wintering grounds may be severe, since even protected populations continue to decline.

**How to Help:** You can be a tremendous help in the success of a plover nest by observing these few effortless rules. Restrict beach activity between mid-May and early August to the lower beach zones (along the water's edge). Keep dogs on a leash, and only use ORVs on designated trails. Completely avoid locations with active nesting pairs posted with signs and fencing. If you see an adult in its "broken-wing" distraction display, you have entered its breeding territory, so leave the area immediately.

**Caspian Tern** (*Sterna caspia*)
State Threatened

Pop. Trend: Increasing
Est. 1989 Michigan Pop.: 2,300
breeding pairs

**Identification:** The Caspian tern has an average wingspan of 4 1/2 feet, making it one of the largest terns in the world. Its large size combined with a short, wedged tail, stout red bill, and conspicuous black cap readily identify this species from gulls and other terns. In flight, the Caspian tern often hovers over water or holds its bill in a downward fashion. It frequently makes a low, harsh call while flying.

**Range:** The Caspian tern is found throughout the world, nesting along ocean coasts and inland waterways. The Great Lakes region harbors around one third of this continent's population. Historically, the Caspian tern was restricted to northern Lake Michigan. Since the turn of the century, populations have fluctuated until the invasion by the alewife in the mid-1950s. This accessible prey allowed the Caspian tern to increase in numbers, which continues today. Colonies are found on six islands, including a new and expanding nesting population in Saginaw Bay. The other five sites are in northern Lake Michigan. The Great Lakes population winters along the shores of the Gulf of Mexico.

**Habitat and Habits:** Caspian terns prefer nesting sites on sparsely vegetated, sandy islands. Recently, a colony was formed on a disposal dike in Saginaw Bay. This indicates that nesting sites can be artificially created or managed to increase numbers. Additionally, this type of management would more evenly distribute Michigan's concentrated population. Caspian terns typically nest in large colonies of several hundred birds. The nest is a slight depression in the sand, frequently within a few feet of a neighbor's nest. Adults will renest if the initial attempt fails early in the breeding season. The Caspian tern lays two to three eggs from May to June. Both adults share in the month-long incubation. Two introduced fish, the alewife and American smelt, are important prey for the Great Lakes Caspian tern populations.

**Limiting Factors:** Unlike its smaller cousin, the common tern, the Caspian tern appears to never have been a widespread resident of

Map 17. Caspian Tern. Distribution of breeding pairs in 1989.

Caspian Tern

the Great Lakes. Although fluctuating population levels are a natural part of this bird's biology, limited island nesting sites, competition with expanding gull populations, and continued human disturbance have caused its threatened status. High water levels, chemical contamination, and predation from mammals also contribute to poor nesting success. The high number of pairs in Michigan is endangered by the limited number of colonies. A succession of catastrophies in northern Lake Michigan (such as inclement weather) could wipe out an entire nesting season.

**How to Help:** Several islands with Caspian tern colonies are protected. Boaters should be aware of the effect they could have on nesting colonies. Avoid landing near them. To compensate for the large gull populations and human-induced changes on the Great Lakes, organizations could provide artificial nesting islands or clear vegetation on existing sites. Consult with the DNR before attempting these management activities.

**Common Tern** (*Sterna hirundo*)     Pop. Trend: Slightly decreasing
State Threatened                        Est. 1989 Michigan Pop.: 1,400
                                        breeding pairs

**Identification:** Adult common terns are recognized by their pointed wings (2 1/2-foot wingspan), deeply forked tail, black cap, and red, black-tipped bill. About half the size of its threatened relative, the Caspian tern, this species appears very buoyant in flight. Immatures have a dark bill and lack an all-black cap. The common tern can be confused with the similar Forster's tern, but may be distinguished by its high-pitched call in contrast to the Forster's low-pitched, nasal call.

**Range:** The common tern occurs throughout the northern portions of the world. Nesting colonies are distributed through much of the Great Lakes region. In Michigan, the common tern was threatened with extinction at the turn of the century. Due to full protection and the bird's biological nature, it recovered to 6,000 nesting pairs in the 1930s. Thereafter, common tern populations have slowly fallen, fluctuating at diminishing levels. Since 1976, the number of nesting pairs has varied between 1,400 and 2,100. Common tern colonies are most concentrated in northern Lake Michigan, the St. Mary's River, Saginaw Bay, and western Lake Erie. There continues to be a decline in nesting pairs. This tern primarily winters in South America.

**Habitat and Habits:** This species typically nests in colonies on sand-gravel substrate and sparsely vegetated beaches. Islands, coastal points, and isolated artificial sites are used for nesting. Michigan's population is restricted to areas along the Great Lakes, although common terns have been known to nest on inland lakes. In May, pairs scratch out a slight depression for their nest. An average of two to three eggs are laid and incubated by both parents for 3 1/2 weeks. The adults vigorously defend the nest, but if unsuccessful, another nesting attempt is frequently made. The young are capable of flight within 4 weeks. This tern's main diet of small fish is typically caught by hovering and then diving.

**Limiting Factors:** Many natural and human-related changes affect the common tern, making it difficult to assess its actual population status. A high number of nesting pairs is required to withstand

Map 18. Common Tern. Distribution of breeding pairs in 1989.

Common Tern

naturally fluctuating populations. Lower Great Lakes' water levels should provide this tern and other colonial nesters additional safe nesting areas. Threatening factors include limited nesting sites, high water levels, inclement weather, gull competition and predation, human disturbance of nesting sites, chemical contamination, and vegetative succession.

**How to Help:** Providing and maintaining nesting habitat is one way to help. Recent research shows that annual brush removal in suitable areas less than 15 feet in diameter will attract nesting common terns. Larger, isolated areas may invite gulls. Creating artificial sites is also acceptable, as long as the soil does not contain chemical contaminants and is formed to withstand inclement weather. In addition, predator proofing nesting colonies is important to consider. While boating, always avoid close inspection of nesting colonies.

**Barn Owl** (*Tyto alba*)
State Endangered

Pop. Trend: None
Est. 1989 Michigan Pop.: No known breeding pairs

**Identification:** This medium-sized owl has a white, heart-shaped facial disk, long legs, and ghostly white underparts and wing linings. The golden back is sprinkled with white and black spots. Mature barn owls have a wingspan of about 3 1/2 feet, and stand 16 inches high. Unlike other owls, this species is generally silent. If disturbed, a hissing screech may be emitted.

**Range:** The barn owl has a worldwide distribution that includes much of the United States. Northern populations in the Midwest and Northeast are declining, but it is still a common resident in several western and southern regions. Historically, the barn owl was rarely seen in southern Michigan. Before European settlement, it may have occupied the extensive prairies and oak savannas found throughout the state's southern 3 tiers of counties. After reaching a peak of what one prominent ornithologist thought as being "hundreds of individuals" in the 1930s, the population declined to only a few pairs by the 1970s. The last known nesting pair was located in Monroe County in 1983. Individuals are occasionally found, suggesting the presence of breeding pairs. Since 1987, barn owl observations have been confirmed in Midland, Monroe, and St. Joseph counties. This species remains near its nesting territory throughout all or part of the winter.

**Habitat and Habits:** Primarily a bird of grasslands, marshes, and other open habitats, the barn owl requires tree cavities or artificial structures for nest sites. As its name implies, this owl has taken advantage of large, open buildings, such as barns, for rearing its young. Michigan's barn owls typically lay five to seven eggs in April or early May. As with nearly all owls, a true nest is not built. Instead, the eggs are placed on an open surface. After a month's incubation, the young spend seven to eight weeks in the nest. Quality, open habitats, such as wet meadows and uncultivated grasslands, are essential for providing an abundant food supply. Small rodents are the primary prey. In fact, this owl's Michigan diet has been found to overwhelmingly comprise meadow voles.

Map 19. Barn Owl. Historical distribution of nesting pairs.

Barn Owl

**Limiting Factors:** The barn owl's survival has always been precarious since Michigan is at the edge of its range. Large contiguous regions of suitable nesting and foraging habitat are scarce. Only recently has the importance of high-quality hunting grounds been fully realized. Prey density and distribution may be the key factors for a viable barn owl population. Converting small, scattered farm fields into large monocultures of row crops is a major reason for its decline. Severe winter weather, great horned owl predation, and secondary poisoning from ingesting contaminated rodents have also contributed to the drastic decline documented in Michigan.

**How to Help:** A management technique with a twofold value is intensive nest box programs. These artificial sites can be used for both nesting and roosting. Crucial to this type of project, however, is nest box placement near suitable hunting grounds. Open habitats with high densities of small rodents are a strict requirement. Report all barn owl sightings to the DNR Endangered Species Office.

## Long-Eared Owl (*Asio otus*)
State Threatened

Pop. Trend: Slightly decreasing
Est. Michigan Pop.: Unknown

**Identification:** Like most owls, the long-eared owl is active during nighttime hours. Its highly secretive nature and cryptic coloration, however, makes its discovery difficult. When found, identify this crow-sized owl (13–16 inches long, wingspan of 36–43 inches) by its overall mottled brown plumage, streaked underparts, orange facial disk, and closely set ear tufts. It has a buoyant flight with quick but deep strokes. This owl's repertoire of calls is varied, including soft hoots, barking calls, and catlike wailing sounds. Although generally silent, the long-eared owl is most vocal before and during incubation.

**Range:** Occurring throughout northern Eurasia and North America, its breeding range extends across much of the United States, south to California, Texas, Indiana, and the Appalachian Mountains. Former and current Michigan nest records are primarily known from the southern Lower Peninsula; by the 1950s confirmed breeding was known from ten southern Lower Peninsula and two northern Lower Peninsula counties and one Upper Peninsula county. Intensive and widespread surveys during the 1980s documented few breeding confirmations, indicating a potential decline. Most observations of nesting pairs and young were primarily in state game areas in the southern Lower Peninsula. Migratory corridors are known at Whitefish Point; standard, mist-netting operations in the spring have annually captured between 20 and 63 individuals since 1983. Northern populations (such as in Canada) shift southward in winter to the United States. Southern Lower Peninsula breeding pairs may remain year-round if food and shelter are not limiting.

**Habitat and Habits:** Two distinct habitat components are required by a breeding pair: large openings for foraging and wooded areas with conifers for nesting. Abandoned crow and hawk nests are used between mid-March to late May by a nesting pair. Only females incubate the three to eight eggs in 21–26 days. Young hatch at varying intervals, leaving the nest at three to four weeks and fledging at four to six weeks. Family units may remain together throughout the winter. Small mammals, especially meadow voles, are its major prey. High rodent numbers, representative in short-grass fields and wet meadows, are crucial for nesting success. In winter,

Map 20. Long-eared Owl. Distribution of breeding pairs in 1989.

Long-eared Owl

conifer stands and grape vine thickets provide favored secluded roost sites. Colonial roosts sometimes reach several dozen individuals.

**Limiting Factors:** Breeding population trends are difficult to monitor. However, loss and degradation of optimal foraging habitat is probably related to local declines. Increased great-horned owl competition, direct human disturbance, and environmental contaminants commonly accompany habitat loss. Recent trends toward more intensive land-use patterns for agriculture reduce the suitability of foraging habitat.

**How to Help:** Protection and proper management of extensive short-grass openings near conifer stands are essential for sustaining long-eared owl nesting pairs. Healthy long-eared owl populations mean managing for high vole densities. Human disturbance in occupied conifer stands during the breeding season and winter needs to be minimal. Migration is monitored at research stations such as at Whitefish Point, but time-effective surveys still are needed during the breeding season. Report all March to July observations to the DNR Endangered Species Office.

# Short-Eared Owl
*(Asio flammeus)*
State Endangered

Pop. Trend: Slightly decreasing
Est. 1989 Michigan Pop.: 1–3 breeding pairs

**Identification:** This medium-sized owl has long wings, a short tail, a tawny body with streaking, and a round face. It generally displays its small ear tufts only when agitated. The short-eared owl's buoyant, irregular, floppy wingbeats resemble a giant moth in flight. Adults are typically 13–17 inches long with a wingspan of about 42 inches.

**Range:** This owl's range is worldwide, although its distribution is widely scattered. Short-eared owls occur throughout North America as either residents or visitors, but populations in Michigan and the Midwest have experienced long-term declines. Formerly breeding throughout the state in scattered local populations, summering short-eared owls are now only seen along Lake Erie marshes, the thumb area, and eastern Upper Peninsula grasslands. This latter location, known as the Rudyard Flats, may support Michigan's only existing nesting population. In southern lower Michigan this owl is more common during migration and winter.

**Habitat and Habits:** The short-eared, unlike many of Michigan's other nesting owls, is restricted to open land. Marshes, grasslands, and pastures are its preferred habitats. Following a spectacular courtship flight display, a flimsy nest is built on the ground. An average of five to seven eggs are laid by mid-May. Although the young become independent in five weeks, family units often migrate together. The short-eared owl is very dependent on meadow voles and other rodents for its food throughout the year. In fact, its population widely fluctuates with the rodents it hunts. The short-eared owl commonly hunts during the daytime.

**Limiting Factors:** The decline of Michigan's short-eared owl population is not clearly understood, and the owl's dynamic, unpredictable nesting habits make its status even more difficult to assess. Many areas of the state continue to provide seemingly suitable habitats, although the low quality and patchiness of these habitats may account for the owl's statewide decline. Midwest studies on grassland-oriented owls, for example, have found that row crops, hedges, and managed pastures cannot support large, consistent rodent popula-

Map 21. Short-eared Owl. Distribution of breeding pairs in 1989.

Short-eared Owl

tions. As a result, these types of open areas do not sustain viable populations of raptors such as the short-eared owl. The best types of open land for this bird are low-use pastures, large grasslands, and marshes. Other factors contributing to this owl's general population decline include poisoning, illegal shooting, and collisions with motor vehicles (from its habit of gliding low over fields and across roads).

**How to Help:** Efforts that could help this owl are limited. However, small groups or organizations can help establish viable breeding populations by protecting or creating large areas of quality grassland and marsh, its optimal habitats. Reporting summer records is particularly important, because full protection and subsequent conservation measures during the bird's breeding season can be immediately applied. Report all May through July observations of this owl to the DNR Endangered Species Office.

# Loggerhead Shrike

(*Lanius ludovicianus*)
State Endangered

Pop. Trend: Slightly decreasing
Est. 1989 Michigan Pop.: 4–6 breeding pairs

**Identification:** The loggerhead shrike has a striking appearance. It is a grayish, robin-sized predatory songbird with a black face mask, large, white wing patches contrasting with dark wings, and a slightly hooked bill. In flight, the loggerhead shrike usually dips up and down, producing a flickering white wing-effect. It averages 8–10 inches long. Its similar relative, the northern shrike, occurs in Michigan from late autumn to early spring. Because the two species are easily confused with one another and may seasonally overlap, identify them carefully.

**Range:** The loggerhead shrike once commonly occurred throughout the United States, ranging from southern Canada to southern Mexico. But several regional populations have recently declined, particularly in the Midwest. As recently as 20 years ago, breeding was confirmed in at least 11 Lower Peninsula counties. However, by 1981, it had declined to a known single pair in Allegan County. Due to an intensive survey in 1987, four nesting pairs were located as were some single birds. Occasional migrants and wintering birds are sighted in scattered locations throughout the state. Great Lakes' loggerhead shrikes generally winter in the southeastern United States.

**Habitat and Habits:** Loggerhead shrikes require large openings, either natural or artificially created. Orchards, abandoned fields, and hedgerows with thorny shrubs and trees are habitat types that Michigan loggerhead shrikes typically prefer. Dense or thorny shrubs and trees, such as hawthorn and eastern red cedar, are favored nesting sites. Between mid-April and late June, the bird lays four to six eggs in a bulky nest that is 8–15 feet above ground. The young become self-sufficient within five to seven weeks, and the adults frequently begin a second nesting. As with other shrikes, the loggerhead captures small mammals and birds without the strong, sharp talons used by raptors such as hawks and owls. To make up for its lack of sharp talons, the shrike commonly impales larger prey on thorns, barbed wire, or other sharp projections. Insects are the preferred prey during summer.

Map 22. Loggerhead Shrike. Distribution of breeding pairs in 1989.

Loggerhead Shrike

**Limiting Factors:** Like several of Michigan's extirpated and critically endangered species, including the short-eared and barn owls, greater prairie chicken, and lark sparrow, the loggerhead shrike's decline is partly attributed to the loss of quality, open habitat, such as native grasslands and oak savannas. Unlike these other species, however, the shrike is not as habitat specific. Studies have documented that it can successfully inhabit small, highly disturbed areas. Additional research is needed to examine other possible limiting factors, such as nesting success rates, competition for available winter habitats, and the effects of toxic chemicals.

**How to Help:** Long-term solutions that may be supported by concerned private groups include the management of thorny, shrubby habitat, funding loggerhead shrike studies, and encouragement of federal listing by the U.S. Department of Interior for the Midwest's loggerhead shrike population. The use of chemicals on lawns and other managed areas should be minimized or abandoned as they have been shown to directly kill songbirds. Report all sightings of the loggerhead shrike to the DNR Endangered Species Office.

## Yellow-Throated Warbler
*(Dendroica dominica)*
State Threatened

Pop. Trend: Slightly increasing
Est. Michigan Pop.: 20–25 breeding
pairs

**Identification:** The yellow-throated warbler, once known as the sycamore warbler, may be identified by its black-and-white head pattern, white eyebrow, bright yellow bib, two white wing bars, and unstreaked gray back. Other similar Michigan warblers have streaked backs. Adults are 5–5 1/2 inches long.

**Range:** Primarily a warbler of the southeastern United States, a small and isolated population exists in Michigan. Although it is expanding in the East and Midwest, it has disappeared from historical locations in Michigan. Always a rare Michigan species, it was regularly recorded and confirmed to nest along the Huron, Kalamazoo, and Raisin rivers in the late 1800s. However, it was probably extinct in Michigan by 1907. Until 1969, only two spring observations were confirmed. Today, the only known nesting population is restricted to Berrien County along the tributaries of the Galien River. Since 1969, one to three singing males were known in this region. However, intensive surveys in 1988 and 1989 discovered 14–21 yellow-throated warbler territories. During these surveys, several birds were observed carrying nest material and food. Since 1988, singing males have been found in Branch, Cass, Hillsdale, and St. Joseph counties. The Michigan and Mississippi Valley populations generally winter along the Gulf Coast.

**Habitat and Habits:** As its former namesake implies, this warbler is partial to the sycamore. In Michigan, mature forested floodplains with sycamore providing a supercanopy type of vegetative structure are the exclusive nesting habitats of the yellow-throated warbler. This is in sharp contrast to southern, coastal populations that frequent oak-pine forests and cypress swamps. Typically remaining in the uppermost reaches of the tree while feeding, this warbler also builds its nest there. One of the earliest warblers to return in the spring, the yellow-throated arrives in mid- to late April to establish its breeding territory. An average of four eggs are laid and hatched within two weeks. The young leave the nest at around two weeks. While foraging, it methodically searches for insects under bark and within crevices.

Map 23. Yellow-throated Warbler. Distribution of breeding pairs in 1989.

Yellow-throated Warbler

**Limiting Factors:** Cutting of selected floodplain forests along rivers, where this warbler's isolated populations existed, caused it to disappear in southern Michigan. In Berrien County, the yellow-throated warbler is restricted to the few remaining forested river valleys harboring mature sycamores. Brown-headed cowbird nest parasitism may be a threat to yellow-throated warbler nesting success. Chemical contamination is another long-term potential threat to this insect-eating species.

**How to Help:** The small and isolated known population could easily disappear from Michigan. Completely protecting and locating other pairs in the state is a crucial step for long-term survival. As preserving floodplain habitats becomes more appreciated for erosion control and water quality values, Michigan's yellow-throated warbler's chance for survival brightens. Report all sightings of this colorful warbler to the DNR Endangered Species Office.

## Kirtland's Warbler

*(Dendroica kirtlandii)*
Federal & State Endangered

Pop. Trend: Slightly increasing
Est. 1989 Michigan Pop.: 212 breeding pairs

**Identification:** The Kirtland's is a large warbler showing black breast streaks contrasting with a bright yellow belly. Its bluish gray back and wings are heavily streaked, and it displays two white wing bars. Its habit of persistent tail wagging also helps identify the bird. Females are paler in color than males. Adults measure 5 3/4 inches long.

**Range:** One reason for the Kirtland's critical status is its very restricted breeding range. Even before the settlement of Michigan, its distribution had been very limited. There is only one confirmed record of this species nesting outside of Michigan—an adult feeding fledglings in eastern Ontario in 1948. In 1971, the total number of pairs dropped to 201, down from 502 pairs just ten years before. Since then, the Kirtland's warbler has been the subject of intense study. In the last 18 years its population has fluctuated between 167 and 242 pairs. This warbler now nests only in a small area of Michigan that includes portions of six northern Lower Peninsula counties, primarily Crawford and Oscoda. Singing males are occasionally found in other areas of the Great Lakes region, including the Upper Peninsula. Five males were found in Wisconsin in 1988. Following its 1,400 mile migration, the Kirtland's warbler winters in the Bahama Islands.

**Habitat and Habits:** This warbler's selective habitat requirements add another factor that affects its continued existence. It requires nesting areas of at least 80 contiguous acres of pine, preferably jack pine, with trees 6–18 feet high. In a concealed ground nest near the base of a young pine, the bird lays an average of five eggs between late May and early June. The young are on their own within six to seven weeks. Because the male is a very territorial, persistent singer, observers can obtain an accurate annual census of singing males. This ground-dwelling warbler relies on insects for food.

**Limiting Factors:** Intensive management and public education programs have alleviated three major problems that once inhibited this warbler's breeding success. These problems include brown-headed cowbird parasitism, human disturbance, and the loss of nesting

Map 24. Kirtland's Warbler. Distribution of breeding pairs in 1989.

Kirtland's Warbler

habitat. Mortality during migration may be partially responsible for the lack of major population increases, although this is difficult to substantiate. Recently, suitable nesting areas are becoming more available, mainly because of long-term habitat management strategies and large burns. Currently, the population is responding with increases in the number of singing males. Continued habitat management by planting pines in a waved-row fashion and regeneration of jack pine following prescribed burns are essential for further increases.

**How to Help:** The best place to regularly see the Kirtland's warbler is on its Michigan breeding grounds, where it is fully protected. Critical nesting areas are posted. Do not disturb these birds during the breeding period. In summer, entrance into these areas is allowed only by special permit or by joining a free, guided tour conducted by the U.S. Fish and Wildlife Service in Grayling or the U.S. Forest Service in Mio. The rewarding experience of seeing these birds on their breeding grounds promotes interest and appreciation for the unique Kirtland's warbler and for the survival problems it faces.

# Prairie Warbler

*(Dendroica discolor)*

State Threatened

Pop. Trend: Slightly decreasing

Est. 1989 Michigan Pop.: 25–35 breeding pairs

**Identification:** Recognize the prairie warbler by its yellow underparts, prominent black streaks on its sides, and olive-green back. Close views will reveal its black eye and jaw stripes and chestnut-colored back streaks. At a distance, look for its behavior of pumping its tail up and down. The typical song consists of 8–14 notes and is thin and buzzy, ascending in pitch.

**Range:** This warbler is primarily a southeastern U.S. inhabitant during the breeding season, ranging west to Oklahoma and north to Michigan. Its Midwest distribution is local and disjunct. Since European settlement and subsequent deforestation, prairie warbler populations expanded and increased. Recently, significant downward continental population trends have been documented, possibly due to loss of scrub-shrub habitats. Its local history in Michigan is similar, expanding in the mid-1900s and recently experiencing declines. Nest records were known throughout the Lower Peninsula but were clumped in the north-central and southwestern parts. Nesting pairs never became established in the Upper Peninsula. Today, this warbler is generally restricted to habitats associated with the dune shoreline of Lake Michigan, such as in Leelanau and Benzie counties. This migratory species winters in Florida and the West Indies.

**Habitat and Habits:** The preferred habitats of the prairie warbler are rarely prairies; in Michigan, large openings with scattered scrub-shrub islands are more attractive. Formerly, the jack pine plains of the Kirtland's Warbler Management Area were used. Recent observations are from habitats associated with sand dune shorelines, oak clear-cuts, and powerline right-of-ways. Look for singing males in these habitats beginning in early to mid-May. The nest of three to five eggs is frequently made in elm trees. Incubation by the female lasts 12 days. The young fledge in 9 to 11 days and are usually independent after 40 days. Insects and spiders are generally gleaned from vegetation for food.

**Limiting Factors:** Subtle changes in habitat by natural succession is the driving force controlling prairie warbler populations. With the

Map 25. Prairie Warbler. Distribution of breeding pairs in 1989.

Prairie Warbler

suppression of wildfires, however, long-term natural disturbance regimes are disrupted. Subsequently, suitable habitat with scrub-shrub growth interspersed with openings becomes limiting. In addition, unnaturally high densities of brown-headed cowbirds, which generally overwhelm warbler nesting success by dumping eggs in foreign nests, probably affect Michigan's prairie warbler population.

**How to Help:** Recognizing this warbler's presence is an important first step for its help. Its distinctive, buzzy song allows easy confirmation. Once an occupied site is found, protection and long-term habitat management plans should be implemented in association with knowledgeable consultants. Report all June and July observations to the DNR Endangered Species Office.

# Reptiles and Amphibians

FEW PEOPLE regularly are concerned with declining populations of reptiles and amphibians, collectively known as herpetofauna. However, this group's ecological contribution to an ecosystem is enormous. Many of us take the early spring choruses of spring peepers and chorus frogs for granted. But, if current population trends continue, we may be without much of our herpetofauna. Collecting and loss of habitat are traditional problems that continue today. However, the latest development of massive worldwide downward trends in herpetofauna numbers is frightening. Acidification, pollution, environmental toxins, ozone depletion: all are possible large-scale threats that may be affecting this animal group. Closer to home, the three listed snakes and two listed amphibians are some of our most threatened species. Each had limited distributions in southern Michigan and most only survive in a handful of populations.

## Eastern Fox Snake
*(Elaphe vulpina gloydi)*

Pop. Trends: Decreasing
State Threatened

## Copperbelly Water Snake
*(Nerodia erythrogaster neglecta)*

State Endangered

## Kirtland's Snake *(Clonophis kirtlandii)*

State Endangered

**Identification:** Among these three species of nonpoisonous snakes, identifying the eastern fox snake is the most difficult. This species (average length 3–4 1/2 feet) is tan with a series of contrasting dark blotches alternating on the back and side. The large, adult copperbelly water snake (average length 2 1/2–4 feet) is easily recognized by its uniform, dark-colored back and bright, orange-red belly and chin. Immatures, until two to three years of age, are heavily patterned. One of the most secretive and smallest of Michigan's snakes is the Kirtland's snake (average length 1–1 1/2 feet). This species also has a reddish belly, but is conspicuously edged with two parallel rows of distinct black spots.

**Range:** Two subspecies of the fox snake occur in Michigan: the western one in the Upper Peninsula, and the increasingly rare eastern one along the marshes of Lakes Erie and Huron, north to Saginaw Bay. Populations also occur inland along the Saginaw River into the Shiawassee State Game Area. The copperbelly water snake, once found in scattered populations in extreme southern Michigan, has drastically declined. Today, only three viable colonies exist; each in protected areas. The Kirtland's snake, which is extremely difficult to locate, has only been reported from about a dozen sites in Michigan. However, reestablishment efforts are currently underway in Van Buren County, and a new site was discovered in Allegan County in 1987. Three Michigan sites are known to contain this species, which also has a restricted overall range and is being considered for federal protection.

**Habitat and Habits:** Unlike its more terrestrial counterpart in the western Upper Peninsula, the eastern fox snake prefers open, wet areas along the Great Lakes shorelines. This large snake is commonly active during the day, hunting in water for birds and their eggs or along the shore for rodents. Eggs are laid in June or July in

Eastern Fox Snake

Map 26. Eastern Fox
Snake, ●; Copperbelly
Water Snake, ▲; and
Kirtland's Snake, ■.
Distribution of viable
populations in 1989.

Copperbelly Water Snake

Kirtland's Snake

brush-debris piles, and the young hatch from late August to October. The copperbelly water snake prefers wooded floodplains and willow-buttonbush shrub swamps bordering lakes, ponds, and slow-moving rivers. Around 200–500 acres of optimal habitat is required for a self-sustaining population. This snake hunts in emergent marshes and wooded swamps during the day, looking for amphibians, small fish, and crayfish. The copperbelly bears live young in September and October. The Kirtland's snake spends much of its time underground, where it eats earthworms and slugs. However, it may be forced to the surface by rain. Although originally found in wet prairies and meadows, populations of this snake have survived in vacant lots in urban areas. An average of seven young are born in August or September.

**Limiting Factors:** Altering and destroying wetland habitats have been the primary reason for the decline of these three snakes. In extreme situations, such as isolated populations, the survival of a snake species is threatened by heavy mortality resulting from road kills. Their limited distributions in Michigan also have stressed existing populations, as has the indiscriminate killing of snakes by uninformed people and illegal, mass collection by animal traders.

**How to Help:** Protecting habitat is critical, although a more influential measure is to educate people about the significant role snakes play in pest control. These nonpoisonous snakes are important components for a healthy ecosystem, and their existence can only enhance our state's rich wildlife diversity. If you locate any of these species, contact the DNR Endangered Species Office.

# Marbled Salamander
*(Ambystoma opacum)*
# Smallmouth Salamander
*(Ambystoma texanum)*

Pop. Trend: Decreasing
State Threatened
State Endangered

**Identification:** The marbled salamander is a striking amphibian, with its dark and light crossbars on the back and its black belly. Adults are stocky and range from 3 1/2– 5 inches long. Slightly larger than the marbled, the smallmouth salamander has less pronounced markings. In Michigan, it is generally deep brown and frequently has obscure mottling patterns scattered on the back and sides. True to its name, this salamander does have a small, blunt mouth.

**Range:** The marbled salamander is most common in the southeastern United States, but its range does extend north to Michigan. Its distribution in the state has been confirmed in only three counties along the lower Lake Michigan shoreline. This small, isolated population continues south along Lake Michigan into Indiana, but does not connect with more southern populations. Only one site (Allegan County) is currently known to harbor this species. Like the marbled, the smallmouth salamander also includes Michigan at the northern extreme of its distribution. This species is restricted to four counties in southeastern Michigan. Generally the smallmouth is a salamander of the south-central United States.

**Habitat and Habits:** Salamanders occur in a variety of habitats, depending on the season. The marbled is no exception. In the spring and summer, adults frequent sandy areas of deciduous woodlands. They may be found under logs or in the underground tunnels of other animals. During its breeding season, low, wooded areas adjacent to ponds and slow-moving streams are preferred. This is the best time and place to find this otherwise extremely secretive species. Unlike other Michigan salamanders, which breed in the spring, the marbled salamander is unique in that it lays its eggs in autumn in areas prone to flooding. The larvae depend on water to develop and transform into the land-dwelling adult. Soft insects and earthworms are the preferred food items of the adult. The smallmouth salamander is more closely associated with moist areas than the

Map 27. Marbled Salamander, ▲, and Smallmouth Salamander, ● Distribution of individuals in 1989.

Marbled Salamander

Smallmouth Salamander

marbled salamander. It typically occurs under decaying logs or in underground burrows near temporary ponds, in river floodplains, and in other lowlands. Crayfish burrows are commonly used. In early spring, adults move to flooded woodland ponds and shrub swamps to lay eggs on vegetation below the water's surface. By early summer, the water-dependent larvae have changed into the adult stage. This hard-to-find species usually remains underground to feed on earthworms, but may surface during heavy rains.

**Limiting Factors:** Both of these salamanders have been recorded in only a few counties of southern Michigan. Suitable habitats within these highly disturbed areas are now small or they have been severely altered. Water quality is another factor. Because of their dependence on water, salamanders are susceptible to various pollutants and toxins—especially the young, which have gills and are completely water dependent.

**How to Help:** Habitat alteration is the immediate factor that needs to be addressed. Forested areas with sandy soils adjacent to lowlands with temporary pools in southwestern Michigan may harbor the marbled salamander and should be surveyed before any disturbance. Likewise in southeastern Michigan, wooded floodplains or swamps should be inventoried for the smallmouth salamander. Awareness for this group of animals is needed, because they are baseline indicators of the quality of our environment. If discovered, report all observations to the DNR Endangered Species Office.

# Fish

OF THE approximately 150 fish species found in Michigan, those commonly caught by hook-and-line are the most familiar. With few exceptions, many smaller fish are referred to as minnows, with little distinction beyond this reference. However, the diversity and importance of this group needs to be understood. Aside from being prey for other animals, smaller fish maintain balanced aquatic ecosystems and provide information on environmental quality. Many of the fish protected by the state's Endangered Species Act include Michigan at the edge of their range. As a result, widespread changes to our state's waters have severely affected the distribution and abundance of these fish.

# Lake Sturgeon

*(Acipenser fulvescens)*
State Threatened

Pop. Trend: Stable
Est. Michigan Pop.: Unknown

**Identification:** The prehistoric-looking lake sturgeon is not easy to confuse with any other Michigan fish. It has a very characteristic body form with a shovel-shaped snout and barbels, five rows of bony plates, and a sharklike tail. This bottom-dwelling fish may reach a length of nearly 8 feet and weigh over 300 pounds, although the average adult length is much smaller. This is Michigan's largest and longest-lived fish. Individuals over 150 years old have been documented.

**Range:** The lake sturgeon is distributed from the lower Hudson Bay River drainage east to the St. Lawrence River and south throughout the Great Lakes region and parts of the Mississippi River Basin. This species is widespread in the northern part of its range, but is declining in numbers and distribution in southern rivers. The lake sturgeon was once an abundant fish in the Great Lakes and its tributaries. But by the early 1900s, their populations were nearly wiped out. Protection and management have since permitted a tenuous comeback for this species. Significant and viable populations currently inhabit the four Great Lakes bordering Michigan. Three major inland sites also contain self-sustaining populations. These include Burt, Mullett, and Black lakes in the Cheboygan River system, the Menominee River, and the Sturgeon River.

**Habitat and Habits:** Large shallow lakes and rivers are the preferred habitat of the lake sturgeon. Spawning occurs around rocky shores or islands in lakes, and in stone bottoms of streams. These highly productive shoal areas also provide the Lake Sturgeon with an abundant food supply of mussels, snails, and other bottom-dwelling organisms. Beginning in late May, when water temperatures are in the upper 50s, sturgeon migrate to spawn in moving water, typically 2–15 feet deep. Several hundred thousand adhesive eggs are scattered on the substrate and abandoned with no parental care thereafter. This long-lived fish first breeds when 15 years old in males and 20 years old in females.

**Limiting Factors:** The decline of this once common species can be attributed to overexploitation as well as destruction of its spawning

Map 28. Lake Sturgeon. Distribution of inland breeding populations in 1989. (Widespread in Great Lakes.)

Lake Sturgeon

grounds by dams, siltation, channelization, and pollution. Dams have a twofold effect on breeding sturgeons. First, upstream movements are inhibited and second, otherwise suitable spawning habitat is severely altered. The destruction of large mussel beds, an important food source, and the accumulation of significant levels of toxins also contribute to its decline.

**How to Help:** Some lake sturgeon populations appear to be recovering from the heavy losses withstood earlier in this century, but other populations continue to decline. Recent stocking efforts and studies are helping to assure healthy lake sturgeon populations in the state. However, due to this sturgeon's late maturity and infrequent reproduction (only once every four to six years in females), it has a low population growth rate and is slow to respond to management efforts. Individuals taken on the spawning grounds in May or June should unquestionably be returned for legal and ecological reasons. Poaching is a problem in some areas and should always be reported to the local DNR field office.

**Lake Herring** (*Coregonus artedii*)      State Threatened
**Shortjaw Cisco** (*C. zenithicus*)      State Threatened
**Shortnose Cisco** (*C. reighardi*)      State Endangered
**Longjaw Cisco** (*C. alpenae*)      Extinct
**Blackfin Cisco** (*C. nigripinnis*)      Extinct
**Deepwater Cisco** (*C. johannae*)      Extinct

Ciscoes, or chubs, are a group of fish found almost exclusively in the waters of the upper Great Lakes Basin. Members of the genus *Coregonus*, they are unique because of their relatively recent evolution within the Great Lakes. Their potential to diverge into new species and exploit the many devoid ecological niches in the Great Lakes has been halted, however, by several factors. These include the commercial fishery industry, immigration and introduction of competing exotic fish, and an overall alteration of the ecosystem to which they had become specially adapted. Since the 1960s, three of the seven cisco species have become extinct: the blackfin, deepwater, and longjaw ciscoes. Shortjaw and shortnose ciscoes are listed in Michigan and survive in restricted, but continuing populations. Only the Kiyi and bloater ciscoes and the lake herring are considered safe from immediate extinction, though the Kiyi's range remains greatly reduced.

**Identification:** Species of ciscoes can be identified by certain subtle distinguishing features, including the number and size of gill rakers and general physical characters (shape of snout, for instance). Attempts to identify ciscoes more accurately have been clouded because some of the rarer members interbreed, producing a mixture of features. Ciscoes are generally sleek, silvery fish with a pointed snout and an adipose fin (found between the back and tail fin). They range in size from 8–20 inches long.

**Range:** Most ciscoes inhabit only the Great Lakes Basin. The shortjaw cisco also occurs through parts of Ontario; while the lake herring's widespread Canadian and Great Lakes range includes many small, inland lakes. The three extinct ciscoes were restricted to Lakes Michigan and Huron. The shortjaw cisco, also extinct in these lakes, is still found in Lake Superior, where it is being studied at the western end. For the shortnose cisco, the future is not as promising; it has disappeared from Lake Michigan and its existence remains tenuous in Georgian Bay of northern Lake Huron.

**Habitat and Habits:** Except for the lake herring, which prefers relatively shallow water (less than 200 feet), all ciscoes prefer the deeper portions of lakes, ranging from 200–500 feet. They move into shallower waters (60–240 feet) only during the spawning period. Thousands of eggs are usually laid in shallower areas that have a sand or clay bottom. All of the ciscoes spawn in autumn except the spring-spawning shortnose cisco. Unlike the other ciscoes, which spawn annually, the extinct deepwater cisco is believed to have spawned every other year. The development rate of eggs depends on the incubation temperature (an optimal 42°F for lake herring), typically requiring several months. Most cisco species mature in three to four years (averaging 12–14 inches long). Ciscoes are plankton feeders, relying primarily on small crustaceans and larval aquatic insects.

**Limiting Factors:** The relationship that existed between the ciscoes and the Great Lakes ecosystem has been severely altered. Beginning in the mid-1800s, the abundant, larger ciscoes inhabiting Lake Michigan were the initial targets of the commercial fishery industry. Cisco stocks from the other Great Lakes were subsequently exploited, including those of intermediate size. Cisco populations became further stressed in the 1940s when sea lampreys invaded the Great Lakes. The lampreys affected ciscoes directly through predation and indirectly by shifting commercial fishery efforts from the all but wiped-out lake trout to the remaining ciscoes. In the last few decades, the introduced and now common alewife has significantly influenced cisco numbers and distribution by competing for its food supply and preying on cisco young.

In summary, Great Lakes cisco populations and their associated ecosystem have been greatly transformed. Disappearance of the larger ciscoes has affected the composition of Great Lakes fish populations. The smallest cisco, the bloater, has rapidly increased and invaded previously occupied cisco niches. Domination by the bloater has caused genetic "swamping" (two species interbreeding, eventually being recognized as one species) of the rarer species and remains one of the greatest underlying threats to the survival of the shortnose and shortjaw ciscoes. Immediate action from both state and federal governments is required to save these two cisco species.

| | |
|---|---|
| **Eastern Sand Darter** (*Ammocrypta pellucida*) | State Threatened |
| **Channel Darter** (*Percina copelandi*) | State Threatened |
| **River Darter** (*Percina shumardi*) | State Endangered |
| **Ironcolor Shiner** (*Notropis chalybaeus*) | State Endangered |
| **Silver Shiner** (*Notropis photogenis*) | State Threatened |
| **Weed Shiner** (*Notropis texanus*) | State Endangered |
| **Pugnose Minnow** (*Notropis emiliae*) | State Threatened |
| **Redside Dace** (*Clinostomus elongatus*) | State Threatened |
| **Southern Redbelly Dace** (*Phoxinus erythrogaster*) | State Threatened |
| **River Redhorse** (*Moxostoma carinatum*) | State Threatened |
| **Creek Chubsucker** (*Erimyzon oblongus*) | State Threatened |
| **Mooneye** (*Hiodon tergisus*) | State Threatened |
| **Bigeye Chub** (*Hybopsis amblops*) | State Endangered |
| **Northern Madtom** (*Noturus stigmosus*) | State Endangered |
| **Sauger** (*Stizostedion canadense*) | State Threatened |

**Identification:** Darters, small members of the perch family, are generally known for their brilliant colors in the spawning season. They can be distinguished from most other small fish by their two separate back fins. The three listed darters are dark and mottled in color, averaging 3 inches in length. Six of our protected fish, the chub, dace, minnow, and shiners are in the "true" minnow family. The river redhorse and creek chubsucker are part of the sucker family, and the northern madtom is a member of the catfish family. The only mooneye found in Michigan looks like an ocean herring, and reaches a length of 15 inches. The sauger is similar to the walleye, but differs with its two to three rows of small black spots on the first dorsal fin, lack of a prominent white tip at the upper lobe of the tail fin, and the wide vertical bars on its side.

**Range:** Within this group of five endangered and ten threatened fish, only the sauger and mooneye are confined to lakes. Confirmed records for these open water species exist in Lakes Michigan, Huron, St. Clair, and Erie. Two darters, the river and channel, do use Lake Huron as well as its tributaries. There are records of the eastern sand darter and pugnose minnow from the vegetated shal-

Pugnose Minnow

Southern Redbelly Dace

Northern Madtom

lows of Lake St. Clair. The chubsucker has been found in seven counties of extreme southern Michigan. Although possibly more widespread than the three southern Lower Peninsula confirmed records suggest, the river redhorse was last found in 1978. The remaining species are restricted to major southeastern Michigan river systems. These include the St. Joseph, Huron, Raisin, Rouge, and Detroit Rivers. Five species have not been recorded since the 1940s: river darter, bigeye chub, ironcolor shiner, weed shiner, and pugnose minnow.

**Habitat and Habits:** Most of Michigan's endangered and threatened fish are primarily inhabitants of streams and rivers. The eastern sand darter, for example, prefers sandy stretches of slow-moving rivers (currently only known in the Huron River), while the redside dace occurs in the headwaters of cool brooks with pebble-lain riffles and shaded pools. For most of these fish, spawning occurs in midsummer. Depending on the species and size of the female, up to several hundred eggs may be produced.

**Limiting Factors:** Because of the specific habitat adaptations common to many fish, widespread disturbance in and around waterways can severely affect populations. Water quality rapidly deteriorates when marsh and near-shore vegetation are removed. Losing these natural buffering agents causes water temperatures to rise and increases siltation and pollution from agriculture and urban runoff. Other sources of pollution such as urban effluents, stream channelling, and destruction of spawning areas by nonnative, common carp heavily contribute to habitat degradation. Introducing exotic fish species such as brown and rainbow trout and the methods used for their successful release also harm these endangered species and the ecosystems they need to survive. Today, most of Michigan's streams are either contaminated with pollutants or contain alien species.

**How to Help:** Retaining green belts along streams and rivers is critical to maintaining healthy waterways and can be applied by many landowners. Although removing aquatic vegetation is sometimes necessary, these areas protect small fish species. For this reason, use chemical treatments sparingly because of their effect on fish populations and invertebrates, which many fish species use for food. Harvesting aquatic vegetation or designating selected areas as aquatic nursery beds are preferred, environmentally sound control methods. Although many of these endangered and threatened fish occur in Michigan at the edge of their range, they are important components of our waterways and must be preserved.

# Insects

FEW PEOPLE would think of insects in the context of endangered species, yet, in some ways, many of them are more vulnerable to extinction than most mammals, birds, or other vertebrates. Insects comprise the largest class of living organisms on earth, and, because of their relationships with plants, they shape the living natural world. Unfortunately, most of our experiences with insects revolves around negative interactions with a small fraction of pest species. Further, attempts to control insects with chemical pesticides devastate many nonpest species and disrupt local ecological balances. The ability of most pest insects to rapidly evolve resistances to chemicals makes the use of broad-spectrum insecticides a cause of long-term loss, and the ecological imbalances such losses create often result in more pest problems.

Insect species are so numerous that their identification is usually very difficult and technical. The identification features described here are quite general and often apply to other closely related species as well. The positive identification of all listed insects always should be confirmed by a specialist.

| | |
|---|---|
| **Duke's Skipper** (*Euphyes dukesi*) | State Threatened |
| **Ottoe Skipper** (*Hesperia ottoe*) | State Threatened |
| **Powesheik Skipper** (*Oarisma powesheik*) | State Threatened |
| **Dusted Skipper** (*Atrytonopsis hianna*) | State Threatened |
| **Persius Dusky Wing** (*Erynnis persius*) | State Threatened |
| **Northern Blue** (*Lycaeides idas nabokovi*) | State Threatened |
| **Karner Blue** (*Lycaeides melissa samuelis*) | State Threatened |
| **Mitchell's Satyr** (*Neonympha mitchelli*) | State Endangered |
| **Frosted Elfin** (*Incisalia irus*) | State Threatened |
| **Regal Fritillary** (*Speyeria idalia*) | State Endangered |
| **Pipevine Swallowtail** (*Battus philenor*) | State Threatened |

**Identification:** Skippers are among the smallest of the butterflies. The five listed skippers have wingspans ranging from 1/2–1 1/2 inches, and generally range from orange to dark brown in color. Northern and Karner blue males are a delicate light blue, females a dark gray color. The satyr is light brown with small eyespots on the wing's underside and the elfin, with a wingspan of 1–1 1/2 inches, has relatively short tails extending from a brownish hind wing edged with gray frosting. The fritillary has a wingspan measuring about 5 inches. The forewings are bright orange and black, while the hind wings are metallic blue with whitish spots. The 3–4 1/2 inch wings of the swallowtail have black upper surfaces and a row of white spots along the edge of the upper hind wings. The underside of the hind wing is an iridescent blue with a semicircle of seven large, orange-red spots and white spots along the edge.

**Range:** The current distribution of these 11 butterflies is severely restricted. Duke's skipper is only known from five colonies in Lenawee and Monroe counties. The Powesheik skipper has a south-central distribution in Livingston and Jackson counties. Both the dusted skipper and the dusky wing have historically patchy ranges in the Lower Peninsula, but both apparently now are reduced to small remnant populations.

The northern blue is presently confined to the middle section of the Upper Peninsula, with a disjunct colony known on Isle Royale, Keweenaw County. The Karner blue, Ottoe skipper, and elfin gener-

Duke's Skipper

Northern Blue

Karner Blue

ally are restricted to southwestern Michigan. The satyr's rangewide population is now restricted to around 12 widely scattered colonies in southern Michigan. Formerly found throughout southern Michigan, the fritillary's state distribution has been severely reduced and its current survival is questionable. The swallowtail only occurs in the southernmost counties of the Lower Peninsula, associated with the small range of its larval foodplant, the state-threatened pipevine (12 locations in the past 25 years). These locations have provided only three recent records of the butterfly.

**Habitat and Habits:** Most butterflies have adapted to specific habitats or host plant types for part of their life cycle. Duke's and Powesheik skippers and Mitchell's satyr prefer sedge wetlands, and are most prominent in mid-July. The Ottoe and dusted skippers, dusky wing, Karner blue, and elfin prefer undisturbed sand prairies and oak barrens, and the Ottoe skipper is drawn to prickly pear cactus blossoms for nectar. The larval foodplants of the dusky wing, Karner Blue, and elfin is wild blue lupine and that of the dusted skipper is little bluestem grass. The northern blue prefers openings in wooded terrain, where its larval food plant grows, the state-threatened dwarf bilberry. The fritillary also occurs on sand prairies, typically adjacent to wetlands where adults are partial to orange butterflyweed. Most of these butterflies overwinter in the egg or larval stages and have one brood annually. The swallowtail is double-brooded, adults fly in late spring, the second brood is in mid- to late summer. The larvae feed on the pipevine, also known as Virginia snakeroot.

**Limiting Factors:** The survival of these butterflies is limited by larval habitat and food supply. Plant species in sedge meadows are essential to the Duke's and Powesheik skippers and the satyr. Michigan is the stronghold of the satyr, where its survival is absolutely crucial to the species. Prairie grasses are required for the Ottoe and dusted skipper; lupine for the dusky wing, Karner blue, and elfin; bilberry for the northern blue; violets for the fritillary; and pipevine for the swallowtail. The disappearance of the regal fritillary from the state in the past few decades is a mystery, although its habitat has been fragmented into smaller patches and wetlands have been drained. In addition to habitat disturbance, the potential overcollection of some colonies continues to threaten the local survival of several species. Suppression of fires also limits habitat for several prairie-dependent species.

**How to Help:** If these 11 butterflies are to survive, their larval foodplants and habitats must be preserved, especially wetlands and high-quality, remnant prairie-oak barren sites. In addition, protection from outlying threats, such as water and air pollution and ecological destruction of areas adjacent to critical habitats, must take place. Habitat management is required to ensure the proper balance of successional plants necessary for their survival. These actions depend on informed involvement from volunteers with time, expertise, and financial support. Education is crucial to rally support for these unique and vulnerable creatures so they may continue to exist in Michigan.

**Three-Staff Underwing** (*Catocala amestris*)　　State Endangered
**Silphium Borer Moth** (*Papaipema silphii*)　　State Threatened
**Leadplant Moth** (*Schinia lucens*)　　State Endangered
**Phlox Moth** (*Schinia indiana*)　　State Endangered

**Identification:** The underwing is a medium-sized moth with a wingspan of 1 7/8–2 inches. It has a brown-gray forewing marked with three wide, dark bars from the front edge to the middle of the wing. The hind wing is marked with orange and black. The borer moth has a wingspan of about 2 inches and is a uniform dull brown; the forewings are heavily frosted with white scales. The leadplant moth is striking, with mottled dark and pale purple forewings, marked with whitish lines. The hind wing is yellow and black, in varying proportions, and its wingspan is around 1 inch. Adult phlox moths are a pinkish-violet color, similar to spent phlox blossoms. Their wingspan is around 1 inch. The identification of any of these rare moths should be confirmed by a specialist.

**Range:** Each of these moths are restricted in their distribution by the range of their larval foodplants. Both the leadplant moth and underwing have larvae that feed on leadplant, a herbaceous species found in dry, sand prairie habitats. Although leadplant has been recorded from eight Lower Peninsula counties, the underwing has only been found in Barry County and the leadplant moth only from St. Joseph County with an old record from Newaygo County. The larval foodplant of the borer moth is prairie dock and the moth has only been recorded in Berrien, Cass, and Jackson counties. The phlox moth is only known in Michigan from two sites in Newaygo and Montcalm counties. Its foodplant, downy phlox, has a much wider distribution in the state, but surveys of other areas have failed to find the moth.

**Habitat and Habits:** The larvae of the leadplant moth are found on leadplant, where they feed on the flower heads. Adult moths also may be found resting on the flowers. Underwing larvae feed on the leaves of leadplant, while the adults nectar on other sources and probably rest on the ground. Borer moth larvae apparently bore into the young shoots of prairie dock and make their way into the root,

Leadplant Moth

where they feed until mature. The mature larvae leave the root to pupate in the soil and the adult moths emerge in late summer and early fall. Adult phlox moths rest during the day on the fresh, pink flowers of downy phlox during late spring. The larvae feed on the developing seed capsules of downy phlox.

**Limiting Factors:** All of these moths need protection because their larval foodplants are relatively scarce and habitats are restricted. Fairly large populations of these plants (leadplant, prairie dock, and downy phlox), are needed to maintain viable moth populations; scattered individual plants or small groups are not sufficient. The fragmentation of populations of moth and plant populations into small, isolated colonies also makes them vulnerable to natural or human-related disturbances. Either could potentially severely damage or eliminate an entire colony with little chance of natural re-colonization.

**How to Help:** Efforts by public and private conservation agencies to protect and manage needed concentrations of larval foodplants are the only means of ensuring the survival of these endangered moth species in Michigan. These habitat conservation efforts need to be vigorously supported by the public. Potential collection of widely known populations may necessitate close monitoring. Pesticide use and artificial lights near these moth populations also must be prevented or strictly limited. Controlled burning needs to be used to manage prairie areas for moth larval foodplants.

**Lake Huron Locust** (*Trimerotropis huroniana*)  State Threatened
**Great Plains Spittlebug** (*Lepyronia gibbosa*)  State Threatened
**American Burying Beetle**
(*Nicrophorus americanus*)  Federal & State Endangered
**Hungerford's Crawling Water Beetle**
(*Brychius hungerfordi*)  State Endangered
**Grayback** (*Tachopteryx thoreyi*)  State Threatened

**Identification:** Recognize the locust as a rather small, usually 3/4–1 1/8 inches long, grasshopper. It is ashy gray in color with white and brownish markings. The hind wing base is a faded yellow followed by a dark crossband and a clear tip. The spittlebug is 1/4–3/8 inches long, tawny colored, and covered with fine gray hairs. It also has dark brown, V-shaped marks on the forewings. The Hungerford's beetle is only 1/8-inch long and yellow-brown with irregular dark markings appearing as stripes on the back (elytra). The burying beetle is a relatively large insect, 1 1/8–1 3/8 inches long. It is a colorful beetle, with the top of the thorax and four irregular spots on the back colored orange-red against a blackish ground color. The grayback is a large dragonfly, 2 7/8–3 1/4 inches long, with an olive-colored thorax that has two blackish stripes on each side. The face is pale yellowish, the legs are black, and the wings are clear with blackish veins.

**Range:** Mostly a sand dune inhabitant, the locust occurs along the northern Lower Peninsula coastlines of Lakes Michigan and Huron. There are also a few records from the eastern Upper Peninsula shore areas. The spittlebug is known only from Newaygo County and Hungerford's beetle only has been found along short sections of two rivers in Emmet and Montmorency counties. The burying beetle is known from several historical locations in the Lower Peninsula, but has not been seen in Michigan since the 1960s. This federally protected species currently survives at only three known sites: a small island on the New England Coast, eastern Oklahoma, and west-central Nebraska. The grayback is only known in Michigan from one old record in Berrien County and a recent, single specimen collected in suitable breeding habitat from Cass County.

**Habitat and Habits:** The locust lives on sand beaches and dunes with scattered grasses. It is reportedly an alert species and difficult to approach. Little is known about the biology of the spittlebug except that it is found in moist areas within sand prairie depressions. Adult spittlebugs feed by sucking fluids from prairie grasses. The nymphs, however, have never been found; they may feed on roots. Hungerford's beetle adults and larvae are aquatic and usually found on the upper surfaces of submerged rocks in streams or rivers. Very little is known about its habits, although it is suspected to feed on algae. The burying beetle feeds on carrion and certain fungi. Larvae mature on a small animal carcass that is buried underground by the adults. Adult graybacks occur in forest openings, often perched on tree trunks. The females lay eggs among the roots of dense grasses and the nymphs occur in permanent wet spots, such as seeps or small pools, where they live buried in the mud.

**Limiting Factors:** Threats responsible for the rangewide decline of the burying beetle, formerly widespread and relatively common in eastern North America, are unknown. Some observations suggest a link between the decline of old growth forests and the beetle's decline, but a definite cause has not been established. Specialized habitats are the downfall of the spittlebug and locust. Hungerford's beetle is limited to streams and rivers, but unknown factors restrict it to localized sections of riverine habitat. The grayback is rare and local over its entire range, apparently because it is a poor competitor with other dragonflies.

**How to Help:** Since little is known about the biology of the spittlebug and Hungerford's beetle, management needs cannot be determined beyond protecting and maintaining their present habitat conditions. Research into reasons for the burying beetle's decline is necessary before recovery measures can be undertaken. The locust's most pressing need is for protection of undisturbed sand dune and beach habitat, especially along the Great Lakes shoreline. Protection efforts for the grayback at occupied sites should consist of maintenance and monitoring of wetlands suited for nymph development.

American Burying Beetle

# Mollusks

THE FRESHWATER mussel fauna of Michigan is rich and diverse. Most species are confined to the southern third of the state. This distribution represents an invasion of southern species after the last glacial period ended some 13,000 years ago. Following ancient river channels, the present mussel fauna unfortunately established itself in what was later to become the most heavily urbanized section of the state. Currently, 10 of the state's 40 or so species are listed as state endangered or threatened. Destroyed habitat and decreasing water quality have been the major factors limiting these listed species. Traditionally, most were relatively rare throughout their North American range. This, combined with the fact that they exist on the northern fringe of their habitat tolerance, has put their Michigan existence in peril.

As a group, snails are generally very small and easily overlooked except by dedicated naturalists. These snails are essentially northern animals with a local distribution established 11,000 years ago. Three of the aquatic species, the acorn rams-horn, deepwater snail, and Petoskey pondsnail are only found in Michigan (endemic). The rams-horn snail group, in general, appears to diversify into many varieties. Some have suggested that the acorn rams-horn is a subspecies of a more common type. The terrestrial species, the cherrystone drop, is a glacial relic land dweller that resides in small populations in cool microclimates of the eastern United States. There are no current threats against the cherrystone drop or the deepwater snail, but their populations in the state are extremely small, and therefore highly vulnerable. The acorn rams-horn has not been found since 1907, even after intensive surveys, and may be extinct. Development in and around the Petoskey area threatens to overrun the restricted habitat of the Petoskey pondsnail.

| | |
|---|---|
| **Purple Lilliput** (*Carunculina glans*) | State Endangered |
| **Catspaw** (*Dysnomia sulcata*) | Federal and State Endangered |
| **Northern Riffleshell** | |
| (*Dysnomia torulosa rangiana*) | State Endangered |
| **Clubshell** (*Pleurobema clava*) | State Endangered |
| **Salamander Mussel** (*Simpsoniconcha ambigua*) | State Endangered |
| **Bean Villosa** (*Villosa fabalis*) | State Endangered |
| **Lake Floater** (*Anodonta subgibbosa*) | State Threatened |
| **Snuffbox** (*Dysnomia triquetra*) | State Endangered |
| **Round Hickorynut** (*Obovaria subrotunda*) | State Endangered |
| **Wavy-Rayed Lamp-Mussel** (*Lampsilis fasciola*) | State Threatened |

**Identification:** To the general observer, mussels can be identified by a combination of size, shell form, and texture, and by color and habitat. Specific identification is possible using the two empty shells when interior shell color (nacre), shell thickness, and the hinge teeth can be examined. Generally, the freshly dead shells found on riverbanks and beaches are the sole indicators of species' presence. The listed Michigan species vary tremendously in character. The tiny purple lilliput, bean villosa, and salamander mussel are less than 2 inches long. The lilliput has a rich purple nacre, the bean villosa a thick shell, and the salamander mussel a thin, fragile shell. Of the medium-sized species, the catspaw, riffleshell, clubshell, snuffbox, and hickorynut have distinctive shape differences and are up to 3 inches in length. Of the larger species, the lake floater is hand-sized, rounded, and thin shelled, and the lamp-mussel is light tan, elliptical, and ornamented with "wavy rays"—true to its name.

**Range:** All the mussels, except the lake floater, are found in the Ohio River or Mississippi River watersheds. Their current Michigan distribution is restricted to the major drainages of southeastern Michigan. The only known population of the purple lilliput lives in a 90-yard stretch of the Clinton River within the city of Pontiac. The northern riffleshell, salamander mussel, bean villosa, snuffbox, and round hickorynut are all found in the upper Detroit River and its tributaries. The hickorynut and snuffbox are also found in a few

Northern Riffleshell

Bean Villosa

tributaries draining into Lake St. Clair, and the bean villosa extends to the upper River Raisin as well. Barely reaching the state, the clubshell has been found in Hillsdale County in the East Branch of the St. Joseph River flowing into Ohio. Also recorded from the St. Joseph River is the wavy-rayed lamp-mussel. This species formerly had a wide distribution in southeastern Michigan rivers, but is now rare and perhaps best represented in the headwaters of the River Raisin. Finally, the lake floater, from sloughs bordering lower Lake Michigan, and catspaw are known only from museum collections.

**Habitat and Habits:** The lake floater is an exception in the habitat it prefers—silty lake bottoms rather than the river environs inhabited by the other imperiled species. Generally, freshwater mussels prefer running water from 1–6 feet deep with a firm gravel or vegetated bottom. Mussels are filter feeders and maintain a position on the bottom to allow an intake and expulsion of water through two separate siphons. Microorganisms are gleaned from the water as food. Mussels move very little and are only able to expand their distribution through a remarkable early life stage as a fish "parasite." The female mussel propels the offspring into the gills and mouth of passing fish. Here the tiny larvae or glochidia clamp on and remain for several weeks or months. Later, the larvae drop off and begin a more stationary existence. Each species of mussel will only "parasitize" a certain fish host. Unfortunately, the host species are unknown for these mussels, except the salamander mussel, which uses the mudpuppy.

**Limiting Factors:** Mussels are affected by the local bottom conditions and quality. All the watersheds in the mussel's Michigan range have been greatly altered from their natural conditions. Siltation, the result of agricultural and urban development, smothers their living areas. Dams and impoundments restrict host fish movement, slow currents, and raise or lower water levels to unsuitable depths. Industrial and organic wastes concentrate in the mussel's body as well as severely decreasing water quality. Many fish "management programs" also threaten mussels. For instance, toxins deliberately released into streams, for later single-species introductions, result in the loss of the mussels' host fish species (many which are poor recolonizers), competition and predation of the host species by the introduced fish, and unknown impacts to the overall ecosystem. Mussels are excellent indicators of how we are treating our environment, because this group's survival depends upon maintaining clean, well aerated waterways.

| | |
|---|---|
| **Acorn Rams-Horn** (*Planorbella multivolvis*) | State Endangered |
| **Cherrystone Drop** (*Hendersonia occulta*) | State Threatened |
| **Deepwater Pondsnail** (*Stagnicola contracta*) | State Threatened |
| **Petoskey Pondsnail** (*Stagnicola petoskeyensis*) | State Endangered |

**Identification:** These snails can be separated by the form of their coiled shells. The acorn rams-horn is about 1/2 inch in diameter, is coiled to the left, and appears to be a "ram's" horn with seven whorls forming a low spire. The shell opening is flared out like a bell. Three cherrystone drops could fit safely across the face of a penny—they are only 1/4 inch in diameter. It is an orangish to yellow-brown animal with an operculum or lid to seal itself within the shell. The tiny shell of this and the next two species are coiled to the right. The high-spired shell of the deepwater pondsnail has an opening that appears to be pinched. It is less than 3/4 inch long. The color of the animal and shell are pale. The Petoskey pondsnail grows up to 1 inch and the shell is a transluscent white.

**Range:** Found as far south as the mountains of Tennessee and several scattered Midwest locations, the little-known cherrystone drop is nowhere common. In Michigan, the only known population exists in the Upper Peninsula's Delta County along the Bark River. The only and last known location for the acorn rams-horn is Howe Lake—a small body of water about a mile inland from Lake Superior in Marquette County. Several isolated lakes in the northern Lower Peninsula have yielded the deepwater pondsnail. It was collected from two different lakes on Beaver Island, a lake in Leelanau County, and Higgins Lake in Roscommon County. The Petoskey pondsnail only occurs in small tributaries flowing into Little Traverse Bay near Petoskey.

**Habitat and Habits:** Interestingly, the land-dwelling cherrystone drop is a member of a group of snails that are essentially subtropical. Accordingly, it occupies well-shaded, leafy, and humid conditions, such as found on the north facing bank in areas of limestone bedrock of the Bark River. Howe Lake, past home of the acorn rams-horn, is a relatively deep, unproductive lake. This species probably occupied the shallows—an environment well populated by snails of this type. The deepwater pondsnail, true to its name, lives among

Cherrystone Drop

water plants from 15–45 feet deep. At Higgins Lake, it was collected at a depth of 40 feet among beds of *Chara.* All these snails are vegetarians that scrape vegetable material using a rasping tongue covered with rows of hard teeth. They are all egg layers. The cherrystone drop deposits eggs in moist locations beneath leaf litter or logs. The aquatic snails attach clear, gelatinous egg masses to water plants. The rams-horn and deepwater pondsnail are capable of self-fertilization (both sexes in one individual), but the cherrystone drop is either male or female. Strangely, this land snail is a gill breather and the two water species are lung breathers. The Petoskey pondsnail prefers small, spring-brook flowing streams. Little is known of its life history.

**Limiting Factors:** These snails exist in very small and isolated populations. Any change in their immediate environs could place them in jeopardy. The cherrystone drop, currently on private land, is highly vulnerable to any habitat disturbance, such as riverside logging or illegal, "over-the-hill" trash dumping. The deepwater pondsnail's life-style demands crystalline waters where light penetrates to great depths and encourages plant growth. Its Higgins Lake location is a popular recreation area, and shoreline development could decrease water quality there. Changes in the Petoskey pondsnail's stream habitat through pollutants, siltation, or water flow would severely limit its survival. The acorn rams-horn may have already fallen victim to introduced fish that took them as easily available food. Its lake habitat is otherwise well protected on a private preserve.

# Extinct and Extirpated Species

EXTINCTION is forever, but what does it really mean when a species is called extinct? By definition, an animal is extinct if it is no longer found in any other part of its range and there are no living individuals in captive or artificial conditions. Although extinction is naturally occurring, the current, human-related extinction rate of species is alarming and much amplified. To environmentalists, extinction means an unrecoverable loss of a species and its genetic information. Recovery plans, designating and acquiring critical habitat, and strict protection measures are all withdrawn (unless the species is rediscovered). In addition to economic, aesthetic, and ecological implications, extinction basically means a species has completely lost its right to survive on an earth where every species has the unimpeachable right to exist.

Since European settlement, six species and subspecies of animals once found in Michigan have been catalogued as extinct. The glaring loss of the passenger pigeon (*Ectopistes migratorius*) is the most widely known. This species once numbered an astounding 3–5 billion birds, and comprised 25–40 percent of the total bird population in the country. Michigan was one of the passenger pigeon's nesting centers and was dominated by its presence. Nesting colonies measuring several miles in length and width occurred in the state's vast, mature oak-pine forests. However, market hunting and massive deforestation severely reduced its numbers in Michigan and throughout eastern North America. One of the last known nesting colonies survived in northern Michigan until the 1880s. The last confirmed Michigan passenger pigeon was in 1898. The last individual died in a zoo in 1914, marking the end of an important component of Michigan's avifauna. The Carolina parakeet (*Conuropsis carolinensis*) is another once abundant U.S. bird now extinct. Although its presence is unconfirmed in the state, it may have occurred in the southern extremes. This southern U.S. species became extinct in 1914.

Woodland Caribou

Three species of fish, the deepwater, blackfin, and longjaw ciscoes are now considered extinct. Found only in the Great Lakes, overharvesting and habitat changes sequentially brought each cisco to its unnatural demise. The cisco family is covered in further detail in the Great Lakes Cisco section. One other fish, the blue pike (*Stizostedion vitreum glaucum*), a subspecies of the walleye that once was restricted to Lake Erie, is now extinct.

Finally, the eastern elk (*Cervus elaphus canadensis*) historically roamed throughout much of eastern North America, including Michigan. Unabated human encroachment decided the eventual extinction of this subspecies. Ranging over the southern half of Michigan, it survived in the thumb area until 1871. The last confirmed record of this elk subspecies was probably in the early 1890s in Minnesota. Today's flourishing elk population of around 1,000 individuals in northern lower Michigan originated from an introduction of the Rocky Mountain subspecies (*C. e. nelsoni*) in 1918.

The term *extirpated* describes a species that is no longer found in Michigan, but occurs in other portions of its historic range. This intermediate category means we can still recover from mistakes made in the past. Most species in this category can still be reestab-

Lark Sparrow

lished in Michigan. The well-publicized release of peregrine falcons is an example of a former resident species now being returned to Michigan's wildlife complement.

The number of extirpated species in Michigan is more difficult to document, but an accepted figure is eight species. Birds that once migrated through the state, but have not been recently recorded, are exempt from this figure. It is appropriate to note, however, that the federally endangered Eskimo curlew (*Numenius borealis*), has historically been recorded in Michigan during migration. Recently, numerous sightings along its U.S. migratory corridors and on its nesting grounds indicate a resurgence of this species. Michigan residents should at least be aware of its historical occurrence during migration.

The most recent extirpations are the greater prairie chicken (*Tympanuchus cupido*) in 1984 and the lark sparrow (*Chondestes grammacus*). Both originally inhabited the extensive prairies and oak savannas of southern Michigan, actually increasing in the state following the clearing of forests. However, the combined effects of intensive farming in the south and reforestation in the north (in the case of the greater prairie chicken), brought about their eventual disappearance.

The original distribution of the majestic trumpeter swan (*Cygnus buccinator*) in Michigan is not fully known. Only one documented nesting is known (Saginaw Bay), but its nesting range did include much of the Great Lakes region and it historically migrated east along the Atlantic Coast. Old accounts of large white birds in the summer probably refer to this species. Michigan's trumpeter swan establishment project began in 1986. Since then it has had limited success, although new release methods are more promising. In 1989, subadults were released in Allegan, Barry, and Kalamazoo counties and a new initiative has brought dozens of eggs from Alaska with the hopes of improving the success of a self-sustaining population. The Seney National Wildlife Refuge in Schoolcraft County and other northern locations are slated for releases in the future.

The widely known and highly endangered whooping crane (*Grus americana*) also had a questionable existence in Michigan. No reliable records exist, but it is known to have nested east into Minnesota and Illinois. Nevertheless, in hopes of widening the currently restricted western range of this species and reducing the probability of extinction, the feasibility of an establishment project in the Seney National Wildlife Refuge, Schoolcraft County, is being studied. In 1989, an adult whooping crane was observed in migration on Isle Royale (no photographs were taken), probably marking the first known record in Michigan.

Of the two extirpated fish, the arctic grayling (*Thymallus arcticus*) has received intensive support for its reestablishment. Once found in several rivers of northern Michigan, it disappeared in the 1930s due to overharvesting and habitat degradation. Since 1987, thousands have been released in northern Michigan rivers and lakes, including the AuSable River where it was best known. It appears that future releases will take place. The paddlefish (*Polyodon spathula*), a large, filter feeder, once inhabited Lakes Erie and Huron but was last recorded in the Great Lakes in the early 1900s.

For the state's three extirpated mammals, each requires a large territory and only included Michigan as the periphery of their range. Each species was displaced by expanding human settlement. The plains bison (*Bison bison bison*), which roamed in large herds, occurred in extreme southern Michigan. Records of their actual distribution are scarce, since it likely disappeared from Michigan by the end of the 1700s. Bison remained in the Great Lakes region in Minnesota until the early 1880s.

Another former Michigan species with similar herding instincts was the woodland caribou (*Rangifer tarandus caribou*). The caribou

Wolverine

has been recorded throughout the Upper Peninsula and northern
Lower Peninsula, primarily as a regular winter visitor. It survived
on the Upper Peninsula mainland into the early 1900s. The last
Michigan record was on Isle Royale in 1926. Prospects of natural
immigration or successful reestablishment into the Upper Peninsula's boreal forest are possible and are being explored by Isle Royale
National Park.

Finally, the wolverine (*Gulo gulo*), has disappeared from the
state. This secretive species probably occurred throughout northern
Michigan, disappearing from the northern Lower Peninsula in the
1880s and possibly surviving into the early 1900s in the Upper Peninsula. Actual specimens of the wolverine have never been
confirmed in Michigan, but detailed sight records in 16 Michigan
counties have been documented. Natural reestablishment is un-
likely, since the closest populations are well north of the Great
Lakes. Recent suggestions of state-sponsored releases have been
temporarily suppressed due to lack of public support.

# Selected References

## MAMMALS

Baker, R. H. 1983. *Michigan Mammals*. East Lansing: Michigan State University Press.

Chapman, J. A., and G. A. Feldhamer. 1982. *Wild Mammals of North America: Biology, Management, and Economics*. Baltimore: Johns Hopkins University Press.

Murie, O. J. 1974. *A Field Guide to Animal Tracks*. Boston: Houghton-Mifflin.

Jones, J. K., Jr., and E. C. Birney. 1988. *Handbook of Mammals of the North-Central States*. Minneapolis: University of Minnesota Press.

## BIRDS

Eastman, J., ed. 1989. *Enjoying Birds in Michigan*. Grand Rapids, Mich.: CES Publications.

Ehrlich, P. R., D. S. Dobkin, and D. Wheye. 1988. *The Birder's Handbook*. New York: Simon and Schuster.

Mackenzie, J. P. 1977. *Birds in Peril: A Guide to the Endangered Birds of the United States and Canada*. Toronto: Pagurian Press.

National Geographic Society. 1983. *Field Guide to the Birds of North America*. Washington, D.C.: National Geographic.

Payne, R. B. 1983. *A Distributional Checklist of the Birds of Michigan*. Museum of Zoology Miscellaneous Publications no. 164. Ann Arbor: University of Michigan.

Terres, J. K. 1980. *The Audubon Society Encyclopedia of North American Birds*. New York: Knopf.

## REPTILES AND AMPHIBIANS

Conant, R. 1973. *A Field Guide to Amphibians and Reptiles of Eastern North America*. Boston: Houghton-Mifflin.

Harding, J. H., and J. A. Holman. 1990. *Michigan Turtles and Lizards*. East Lansing: Michigan State University Cooperative Extension Service.

Holman, A., J. H. Harding, M. M. Hensley, and G. R. Dudderar. 1989. *Michigan Snakes*. East Lansing: Michigan State University Cooperative Extension Service.

## FISH

Eddy, S., and J. C. Underhill. 1978. *How to Know the Freshwater Fishes*. Dubuque, Iowa: William C. Brown.

Hubbs, C. L., and K. F. Lagler. 1974. *Fishes of the Great Lakes Region*. Ann Arbor: University of Michigan Press.

Scott, W. B., and E. H. Crossman. 1973. *Freshwater Fishes of Canada*. Bulletin no. 184. Ottawa: Fisheries Research Board of Canada.

Thompson, P. 1985. *Thompson's Guide to Freshwater Fishes*. Boston: Houghton-Mifflin.

## INVERTEBRATES

Clarke, A. H. 1981. *The Freshwater Molluscs of Canada*. Ottawa: National Museum of Natural Science.

Covell, A. 1984. *A Field Guide to the Moths*. Boston: Houghton-Mifflin.

Parmalee, P. W. 1967. *The Freshwater Mussels of Illinois*. Population Science Series, vol. 8. Springfield, Ill.: Illinois State Museum.

Pyle, R. M. 1986. *The Audubon Society Field Guide to North American Butterflies*. New York: Knopf.

Jaques, H. E. 1951. *How to Know the Beetles*. Dubuque, Iowa: William C. Brown.

## GENERAL REFERENCES

Cadieux, C. 1981. *These are the Endangered*. Washington, D. C.: Stone Wall Press.

Ehrlich, P., and A. Ehrlich. 1981. *Extinction: The Causes and Consequences of the Disappearance of Species*. New York: Ballantine Books.

Mathisen, P. 1987. *Wildlife in America*. New York: Viking Press.

Myers, N., ed. 1984. *Gaia: An Atlas of Planet Management*. Garden City, N.Y.: Anchor Press.

Nilsson, G. 1986. *The Endangered Species Handbook*. Washington, D. C.: Animal Welfare Institute.

Terborgh, J. 1989. *Where Have All the Birds Gone?* Princeton, N.J.: Princeton University Press.

# List of Endangered and
# Threatened Wildlife in Michigan

## MAMMALS

| Endangered | Threatened | Extirpated | Extinct |
|---|---|---|---|
| Gray wolf | Least shrew | Wolverine | Eastern elk |
| Cougar | Marten | Bison | |
| Lynx | Prairie vole | Woodland caribou | |
| Indiana bat | | | |

## BIRDS

| Endangered | Threatened | Extirpated | Extinct |
|---|---|---|---|
| Short-eared owl | Red-shouldered hawk | Lark sparrow | Passenger pigeon |
| Piping plover | Least bittern | Trumpeter swan | |
| Kirtland's warbler | Yellow-throated warbler | Greater prairie chicken | |
| Peregrine falcon | Merlin | | |
| Loggerhead shrike | Common loon | | |
| King rail | Bald eagle | | |
| Barn owl | Osprey | | |
| | Common tern | | |
| | Caspian tern | | |
| | Yellow rail | | |
| | Prairie warbler | | |
| | Long-eared owl | | |

## REPTILES AND AMPHIBIANS

| Endangered | Threatened | Extirpated | Extinct |
|---|---|---|---|
| Kirtland's snake<br>Copperbelly water<br>  snake<br>Smallmouth<br>  salamander | Eastern fox snake<br>Marbled<br>  salamander | | |

## FISH

| Endangered | Threatened | Extirpated | Extinct |
|---|---|---|---|
| Shortnose cisco<br>Bigeye chub<br>Northern madtom<br>River darter<br>Ironcolor shiner<br>Weed shiner | Lake sturgeon<br>Eastern sand darter<br>Redside dace<br>Lake herring<br>Shortjaw cisco<br>Creek chubsucker<br>Mooneye<br>Silver shiner<br>Southern redbelly<br>  dace<br>Pugnose minnow<br>Sauger<br>River redhorse<br>Channel darter | Paddlefish<br>Arctic grayling | Longjaw cisco<br>Deepwater cisco<br>Blackfin cisco<br>Blue pike |

## INSECTS

| Endangered | Threatened | Extirpated | Extinct |
|---|---|---|---|
| Hungerford's<br>  crawling water<br>  beetle<br>Three-staff<br>  underwing<br>American burying<br>  beetle<br>Leadplant moth<br>Regal fritillary<br>Phlox moth<br>Mitchell's satyr | Duke's skipper<br><br>Ottoe skipper<br><br>Dusted skipper<br><br>Persius dusky wing<br>Frosted elfin<br>Northern blue<br>Karner blue | | |

## INSECTS

| Endangered | Threatened | Extirpated | Extinct |
| --- | --- | --- | --- |
| | Powesheik skipper | | |
| | Pipevine swallowtail | | |
| | Silphium borer moth | | |
| | Great Plains spittlebug | | |
| | Lake Huron locust | | |
| | Grayback | | |

## MOLLUSKS

| Endangered | Threatened | Extirpated | Extinct |
| --- | --- | --- | --- |
| Purple lilliput | Lake floater | | |
| Catspaw | | | |
| Northern riffleshell | Wavy-rayed lamp-mussel | | |
| Snuffbox | Cherrystone drop | | |
| Clubshell | Deepwater pondsnail | | |
| Salamander mussel | | | |
| Bean villosa | | | |
| Round hickorynut | | | |
| Acorn rams-horn | | | |
| Petoskey pondsnail | | | |